At Sylvan, we believe reading is one of life's most important and enriching abilities, and we're glad you've chosen our resources to help your child build these critically important skills. We know that the time you spend with your child reinforcing the lessons learned in school will contribute to his love of reading. This love of reading will translate into academic achievement. A successful reader is ready for the world around him, ready to do research, ready to experience the world of literature, and prepared to make the connections necessary to achieve in school and in life.

We use a research-based, step-by-step process in teaching reading at Sylvan that includes thought-provoking reading selections and activities. As students increase their success as readers they become more confident. With increasing confidence, students build even more success. Our Sylvan workbooks are designed to help you to help your child build the skills and confidence that will contribute to your child's success in school.

We're excited to partner with you to support the development of confident, well-prepared independent learners!

The Sylvan Team

Sylvan Learning Center.
Unleash your child's potential here.

No matter how big or small the academic challenge, every child has the ability to learn. But sometimes children need help making it happen. Sylvan believes every child has the potential to do great things. And we know better than anyone else how to tap into that academic potential so that a child's future really is full of possibilities. Sylvan Learning Center is the place where your child can build and master the learning skills needed to succeed and unlock the potential you know is there.

The proven, personalized approach of our in-center programs deliver unparalleled results that other supplemental education services simply can't match. Your child's achievements will be seen not only in test scores and report cards but outside the classroom as well. And when he starts achieving his full potential, everyone will know it. You will see a new level of confidence come through in everything he does and every interaction he has.

How can Sylvan's personalized in-center approach help your child unleash his potential?

• Starting with our exclusive Sylvan Skills Assessment®, we pinpoint your child's exact academic needs.

• Then we develop a customized learning plan designed to achieve your child's academic goals.

• Through our method of skill mastery, your child will not only learn and master every skill in his personalized plan, he will be truly motivated and inspired to achieve his full potential.

To get started, simply contact your local Sylvan Learning Center to set up an appointment. And to learn more about Sylvan and our innovative in-center programs, call 1-800-EDUCATE or visit www.SylvanLearning.com. *With over 850 locations in North America, there is a Sylvan Learning Center near you!*

Kindergarten
Jumbo Language Arts Success
Workbook

Published in the United States by Random House, Inc., New York, and in Canada by Random House of Canada Limited, Toronto.

This book was previously published with the title *Kindergarten Language Arts Success* as a trade paperback by Sylvan Learning, Inc., an imprint of Penguin Random House LLC, in 2009.

www.sylvanlearning.com

Created by Smarterville Productions LLC
Producer: TJ Trochlil McGreevy
Producer & Editorial Direction: The Linguistic Edge
Writers: Margaret Crocker (Alphabet Activities), Erin Lassiter (Reading Readiness and Beginning Word Games)
Cover and Interior Illustrations: Duendes del Sur
Layout and Art Direction: SunDried Penguin
Art Manager: Adina Ficano

First Edition

ISBN: 978-0-375-43029-9

Library of Congress Cataloging-in-Publication Data available upon request.

This book is available at special discounts for bulk purchases for sales promotions or premiums. For more information, write to Special Markets/Premium Sales, 1745 Broadway, MD 6-2, New York, New York 10019 or e-mail specialmarkets@randomhouse.com.

PRINTED IN CHINA

10 9

Alphabet Activities Contents

Reading Readiness Contents

Beginning Word Games Contents

Kindergarten
Alphabet Activities

The Letter Aa

Practice the Letter A

TRACE the uppercase letter A.
Start at the green arrow.

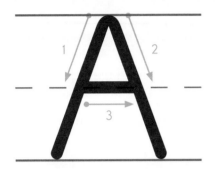

A̲nt

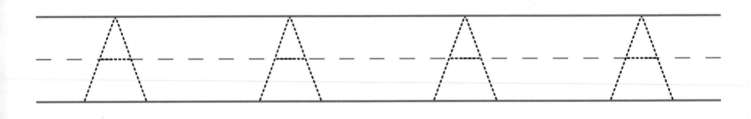

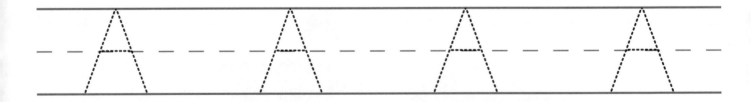

Now WRITE three uppercase As.

1   2   3

2

Practice the Letter a

TRACE the lowercase letter **a**.
Start at the green arrow.

1
2

a

alligator

Now WRITE three lowercase **a**s.

1   2   3

The Letter Aa

Match the Letters

FIND the lowercase **a**. DRAW a line from the uppercase **A** to the lowercase **a**.

A

g   a   a   c   p

Now COLOR the ants that are wearing lowercase **a**s.

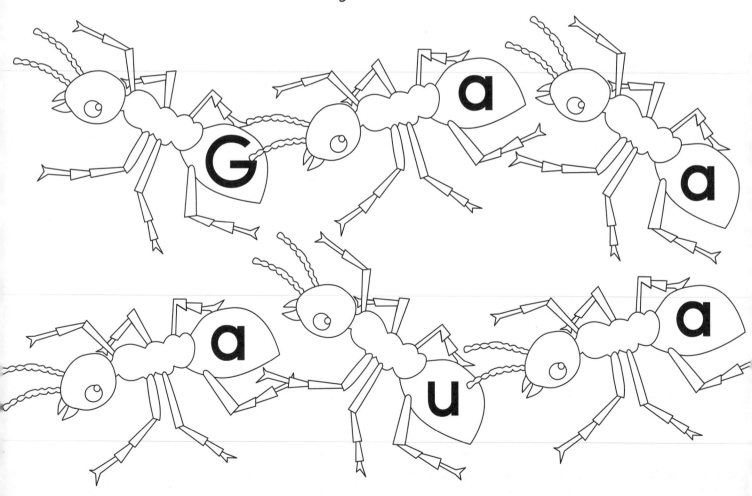

Maze Crazy!

DRAW a line through the path marked with **A** and **a** to get to the apple.
Start at the blue arrow.

Practice the Letter B

TRACE the uppercase letter **B**.
Start at the green arrow.

2

1

3

B

Butterfly

B — B — B — B —

B — B — B — B —

Now WRITE three uppercase **B**s.

B

1   2   3

Practice the Letter b

TRACE the lowercase letter **b**.
Start at the green arrow.

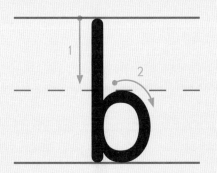

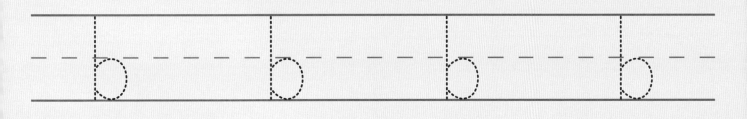

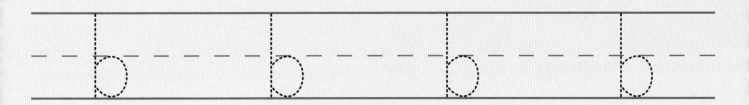

Now WRITE three lowercase **b**s.

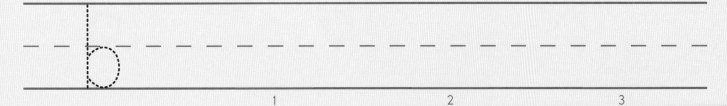

Match the Letters

FIND the lowercase **b**. DRAW a line from the uppercase **B** to the lowercase **b**.

B

x   g   b   k

Now COLOR the butterflies that are wearing lowercase **b**s.

Hide and Seek

CIRCLE the things in the picture that start with **B**.

The Letter Cc

Practice the Letter C

TRACE the uppercase letter C.
Start at the green arrow.

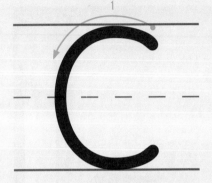

Cow

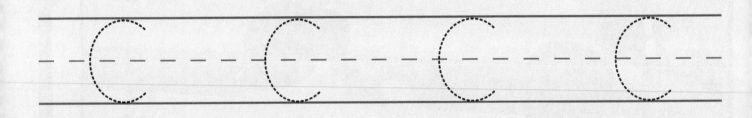

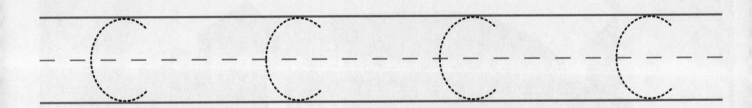

Now WRITE three uppercase Cs.

1   2   3

Practice the Letter c

TRACE the lowercase letter **c**.
Start at the green arrow.

1

c

cupcake

c   c   c   c

c   c   c   c

Now WRITE three lowercase **c**s.

c

1   2   3

The Letter Cc

Letter Draw

DRAW five things that start with C.

C c

Alphabet Art

COLOR the spaces that show C or c.

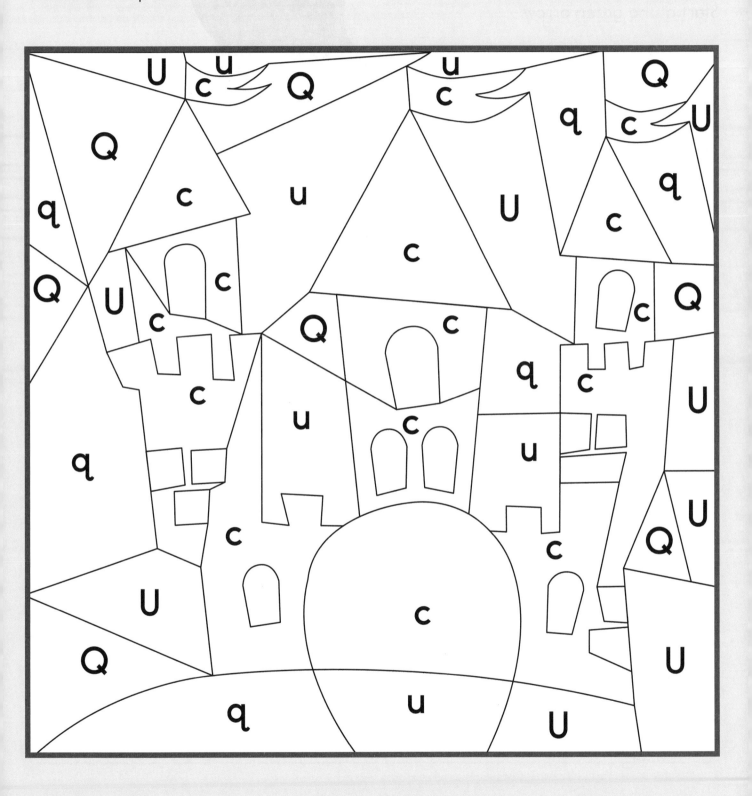

The Letter Dd

Practice the Letter D

TRACE the uppercase letter **D**.
Start at the green arrow.

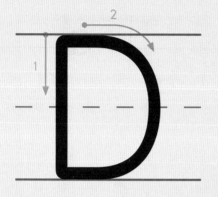

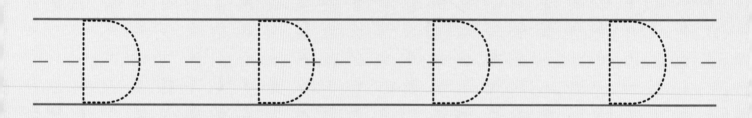

Dog

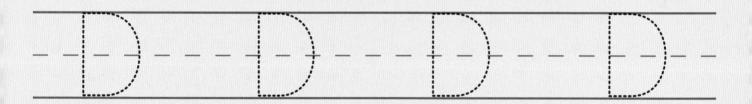

Now WRITE three uppercase **D**s.

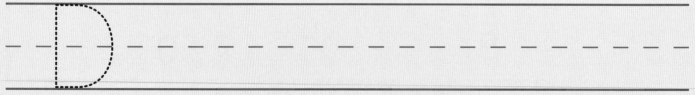

1   2   3

Practice the Letter d

TRACE the lowercase letter **d**.
Start at the green arrow.

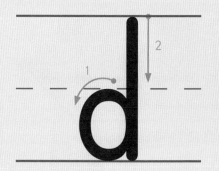

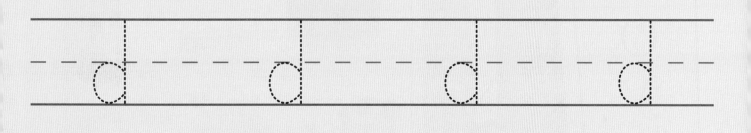

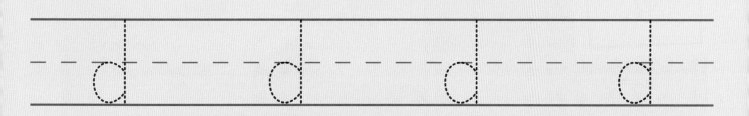

Now WRITE three lowercase **d**s.

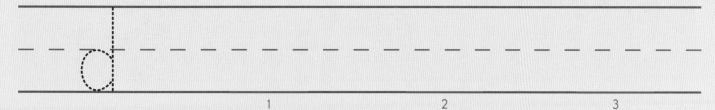

1   2   3

The Letter Dd

Hide and Seek

CIRCLE the things in the picture that start with **D**.

Finish the Word

FILL IN the blanks with **d** to finish the words. The letter may be at the beginning, middle, or end of the word.

1 ___ress

2 ___uck

3 ___ragon

4 han___

5 re___

6 can___y

The Letter Ee

Practice the Letter E

TRACE the uppercase letter E.
Start at the green arrow.

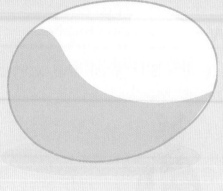

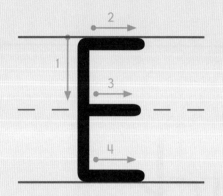

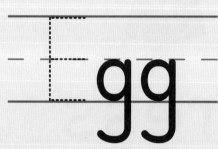

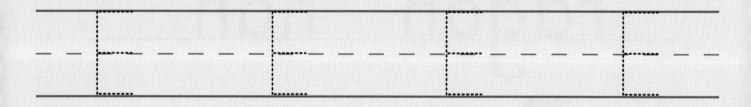

Now WRITE three uppercase **E**s.

1   2   3

Practice the Letter e

TRACE the lowercase letter **e**.
Start at the green arrow.

e

elephant

e · e · e · e

e · e · e · e

Now WRITE three lowercase **e**s.

e

1   2   3

The Letter Ee

Match the Letters

FIND the lowercase **e**. DRAW a line from the uppercase **E** to the lowercase **e**.

E

a e c u

Now COLOR the elephants that are wearing lowercase **e**s.

Maze Crazy!

DRAW a line through the path marked with **E** and **e** to get to the envelope.
Start at the orange arrow.

The Letter Ff

Practice the Letter F

TRACE the uppercase letter F.
Start at the green arrow.

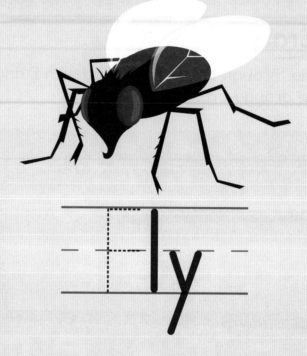

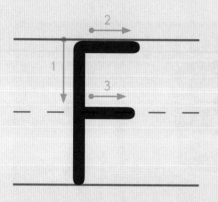

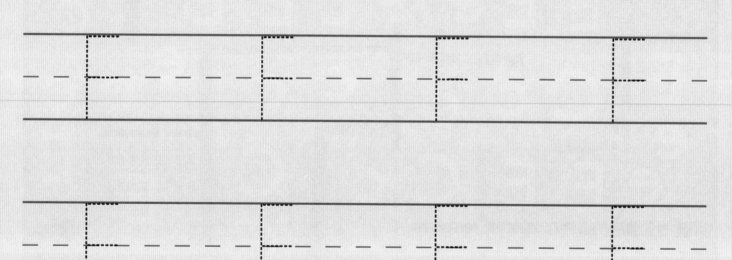

Now WRITE three uppercase Fs.

1   2   3

Practice the Letter f

TRACE the lowercase letter **f**.
Start at the green arrow.

fireman

Now WRITE three lowercase **f**s.

1	2	3

The Letter Ff

Alphabet Art

COLOR the spaces that show **F** or **f**.

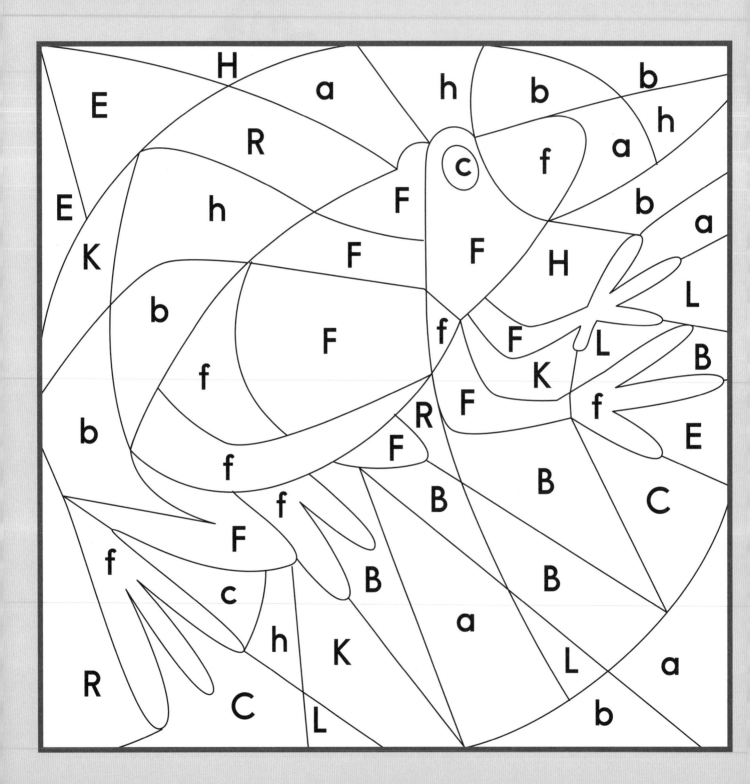

Circle the Picture

CIRCLE the pictures that start with **F**.

The Letter Gg

Practice the Letter G

TRACE the uppercase letter G.
Start at the green arrow.

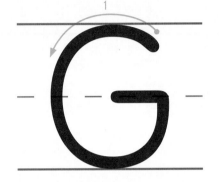

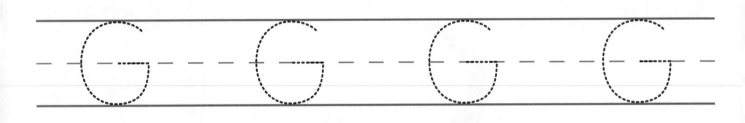

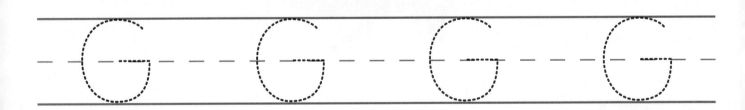

Now WRITE three uppercase Gs.

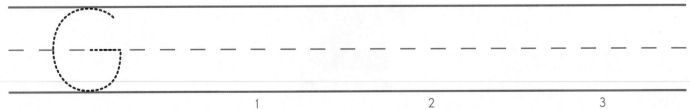

1   2   3

Practice the Letter g

TRACE the lowercase letter **g**.
Start at the green arrow.

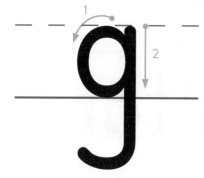

Now WRITE three lowercase **g**s.

1   2   3

Finish the Word

FILL IN the blanks with **g** to finish the words. The letter may be at the beginning, middle, or end of the word.

1
rapes

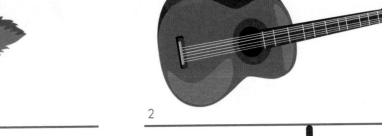

2
uitar

3
ift

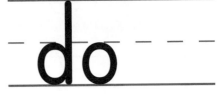

4
do

5
fin er

6
alli ator

Maze Crazy!

DRAW a line through the path marked with **G** and **g** to get to the grapes.
Start at the blue arrow.

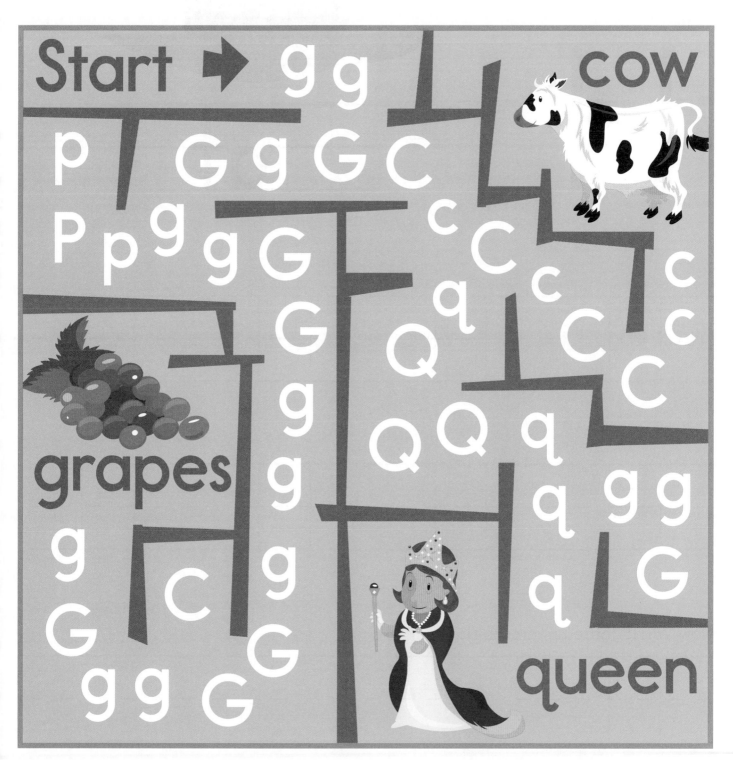

The Letter Hh

Practice the Letter H

TRACE the uppercase letter **H**.
Start at the green arrow.

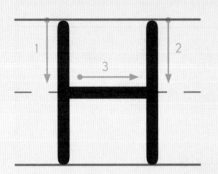

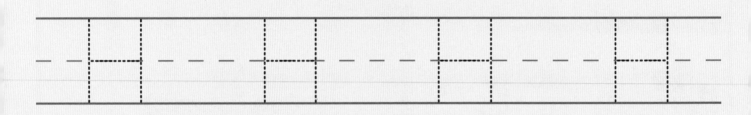

Now WRITE three uppercase **H**s.

1   2   3

Practice the Letter h

TRACE the lowercase letter **h**.
Start at the green arrow.

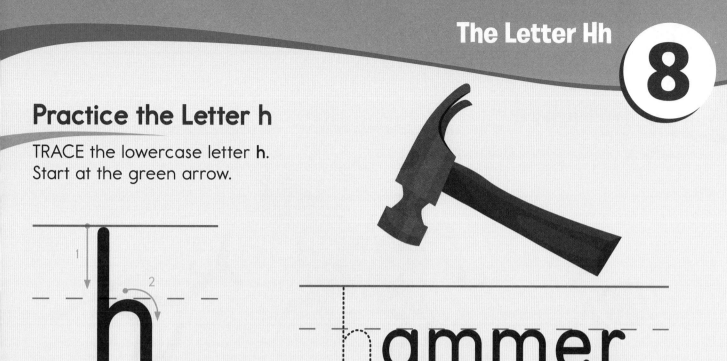

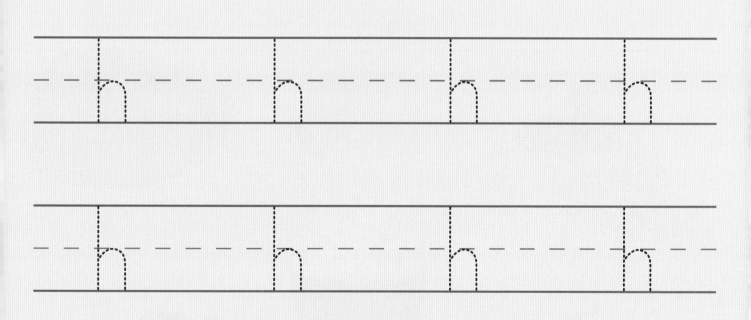

Now WRITE three lowercase **h**s.

1   2   3

The Letter Hh

Circle the Picture

CIRCLE the pictures that start with H.

Alphabet Art

COLOR the spaces that show **H** or **h**.

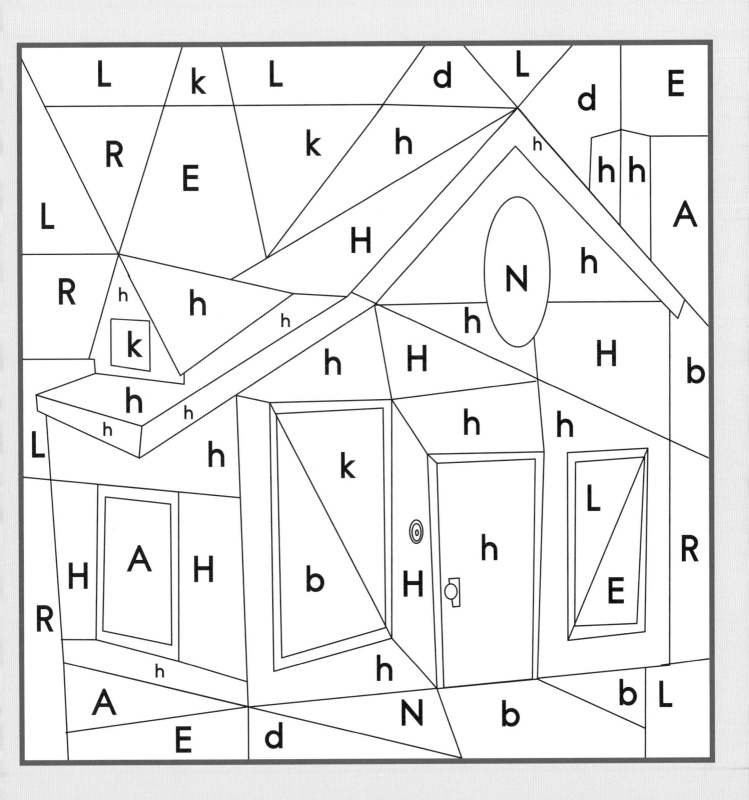

The Letter Ii

Practice the Letter I

TRACE the uppercase letter **I**.
Start at the green arrow.

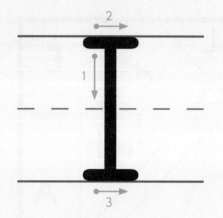

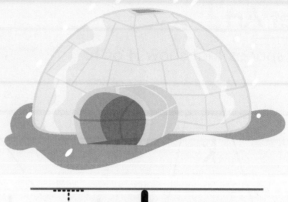

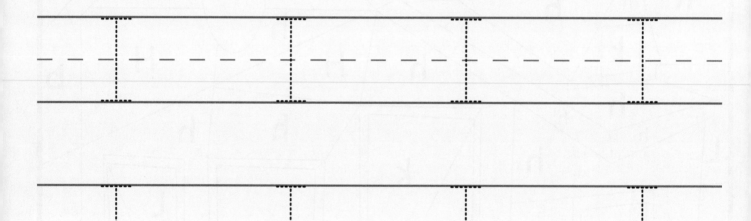

Igloo

Now WRITE three uppercase **I**s.

1   2   3

Practice the Letter i

TRACE the lowercase letter i.
Start at the green arrow.

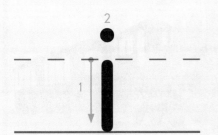

```
2
•
1
i
```

ce

Now WRITE three lowercase is.

i

1   2   3

The Letter Ii

Maze Crazy!

DRAW a line through the path marked with **I** and **i** to get to the ice cream.
Start at the orange arrow.

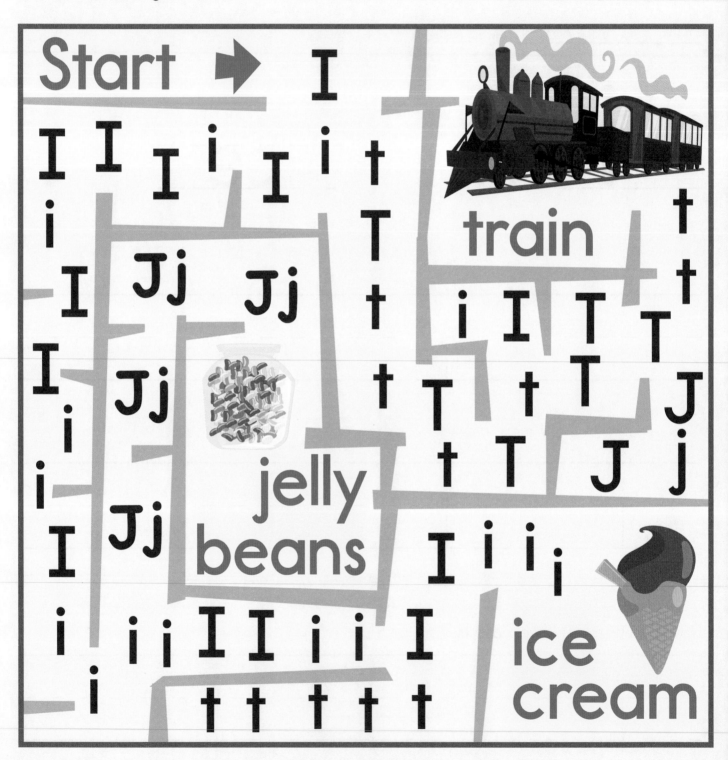

Start ➡ I

train

jelly beans

ice cream

Match the Letters

FIND the lowercase **i**. DRAW a line to match the uppercase **I** with the lowercase **i**.

I

j   **f**   **q**   **i**

Now COLOR the igloos that are wearing lowercase **i**s.

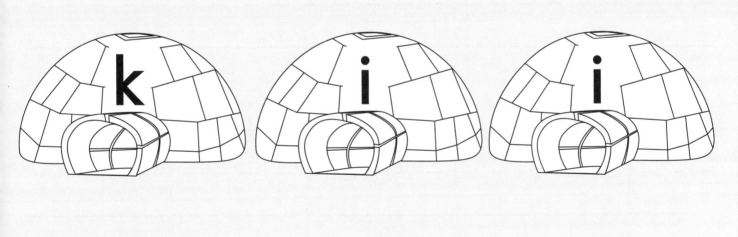

The Letter Jj

Practice the Letter J

TRACE the uppercase letter **J**.
Start at the green arrow.

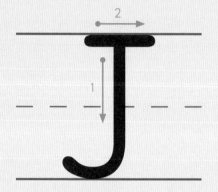

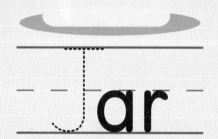

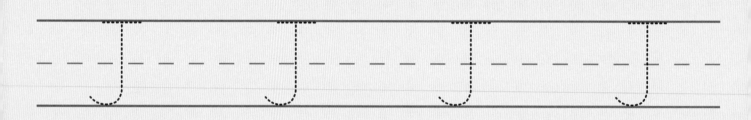

Now WRITE three uppercase **J**s.

1   2   3

Practice the Letter j

TRACE the lowercase letter j.
Start at the green arrow.

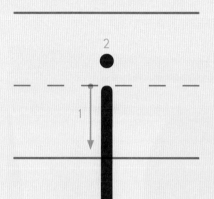

j̇acket

Now WRITE three lowercase js.

The Letter Jj

Hide and Seek

CIRCLE the things in the picture that start with **J**.

40

Finish the Word

FILL IN the blanks with **j** to finish the words.

1 _____
_ _ _ _ _ _ _ _ uice

2 _____
_ _ _ _ _ _ _ acket

3 _____
_ _ _ _ et

4 _____
_ _ _ _ _ ellyfish

5 _____
_ _ _ _ ump rope

6 _____
_ _ _ _ ar

The Letter Kk

Practice the Letter K

TRACE the uppercase letter K.
Start at the green arrow.

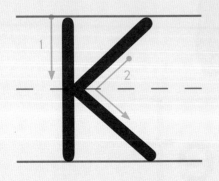

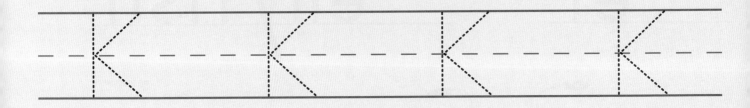

Now WRITE three uppercase Ks.

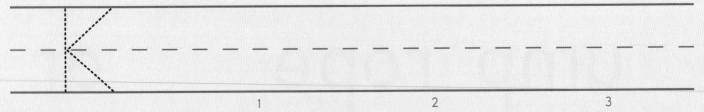

42

Practice the Letter k

TRACE the lowercase letter **k**.
Start at the green arrow.

kite

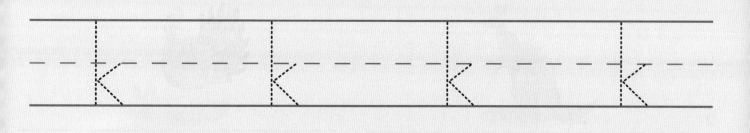

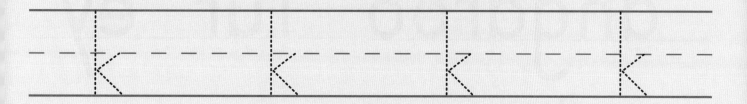

Now WRITE three lowercase **k**s.

1   2   3

The Letter Kk

Finish the Word

FILL IN the blanks with **k** to finish the words. The letter may be at the beginning, middle, or end of the word.

1

___itten

2

___ing

3

___angaroo

4

tur___ey

5

mon___ey

6

duc___

Alphabet Art

COLOR the spaces that show K or k.

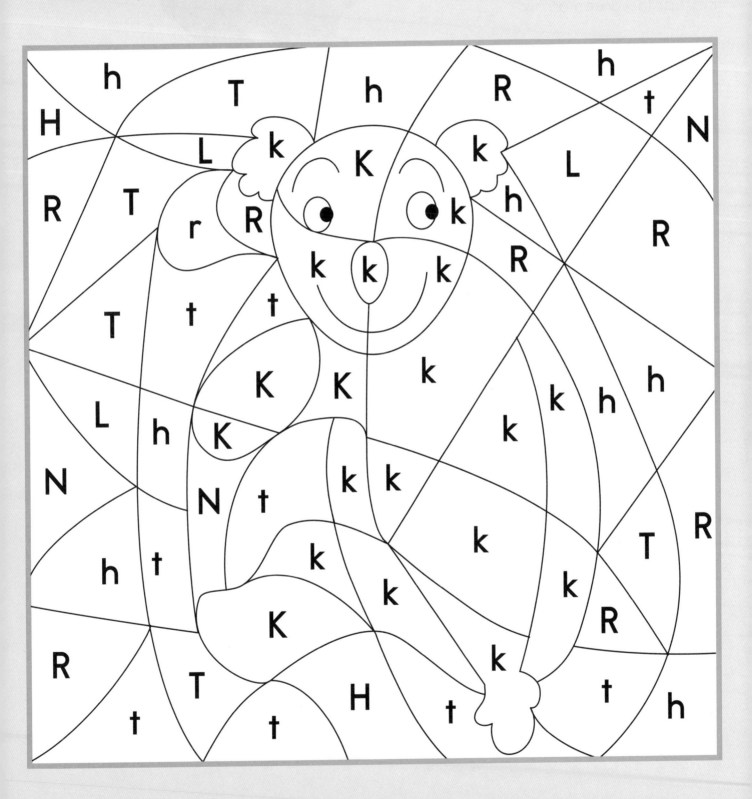

Practice the Letter L

TRACE the uppercase letter L.
Start at the green arrow.

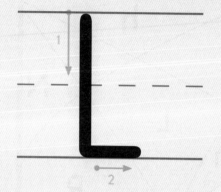

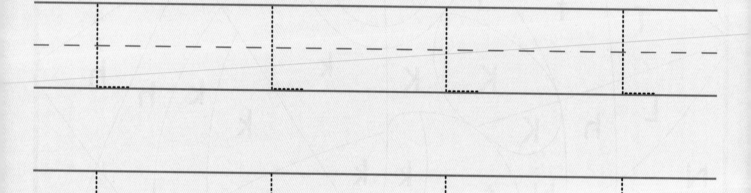

Lion

Now WRITE three uppercase Ls.

1   2   3

Practice the Letter l

TRACE the lowercase letter l.
Start at the green arrow.

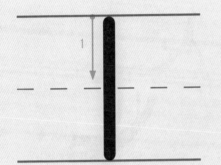

lobster

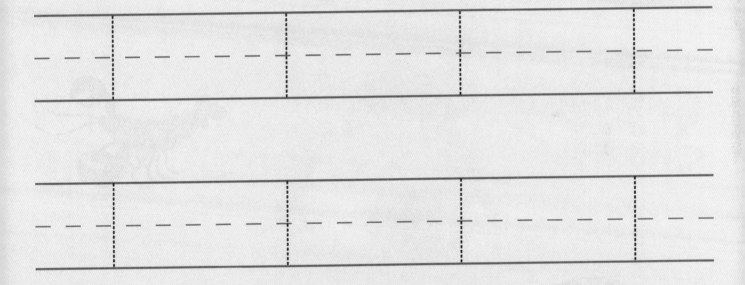

Now WRITE three lowercase ls.

1   2   3

The Letter Ll

Circle the Picture

CIRCLE the pictures that start with L.

Maze Crazy!

DRAW a line through the path marked with **L** and **I** to get to the lamb.
Start at the blue arrow.

Start ➤ L I L L

tractor

ice

lamb

The Letter Mm

Practice the Letter M

TRACE the uppercase letter **M**.
Start at the green arrow.

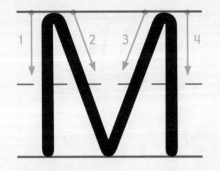

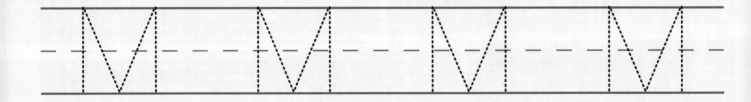

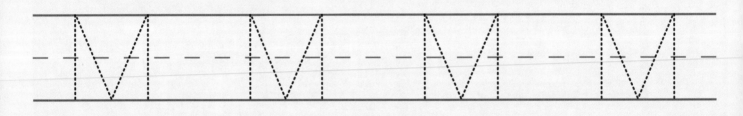

Now WRITE three uppercase **M**s.

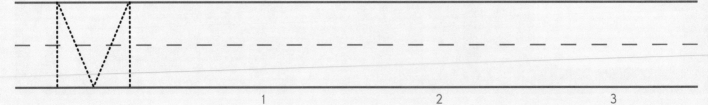

Practice the Letter m

TRACE the lowercase letter **m**.
Start at the green arrow.

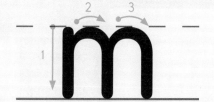

mitten

Now WRITE three lowercase **m**s.

1   2   3

Letter Draw

DRAW five things that start with M.

Mm

Finish the Word

FILL IN the blanks with **m** to finish the words. The letter may be at the beginning, middle, or end of the word.

1
_ailbox

2
_ouse

3
_ilk

4
snow _an

5
ha_ _er

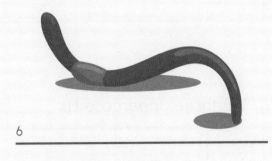

6
wor_

The Letter Nn

Practice the Letter N

TRACE the uppercase letter **N**.
Start at the green arrow.

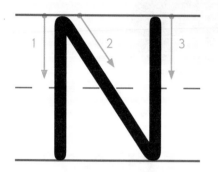

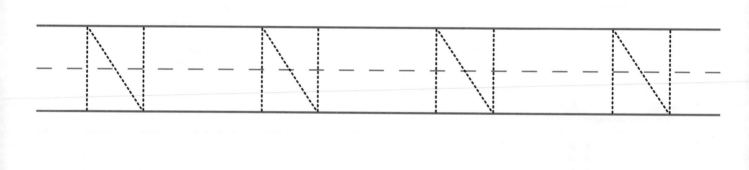

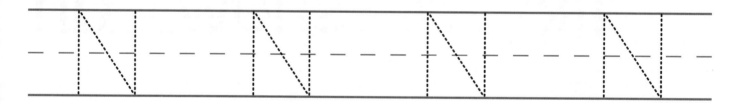

Now WRITE three uppercase **N**s.

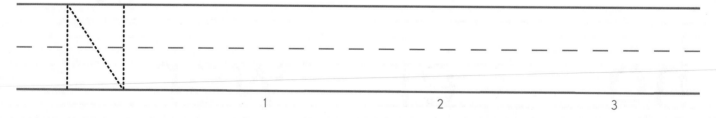

Practice the Letter n

TRACE the lowercase letter **n**.
Start at the green arrow.

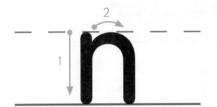

n ose

Now WRITE three lowercase **n**s.

1   2   3

The Letter Nn

Finish the Word

FILL IN the blanks with **n** to finish the words. The letter may be at the beginning, middle, or end of the word.

1

___ ail

2

ki ___ g

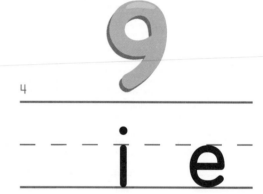

3

___ est

4

___ i ___ e

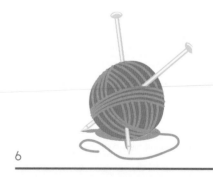

5

u ___ icor ___

6

yar ___

Hide and Seek

CIRCLE the things in the picture that start with **N**.

The Letter Oo

Practice the Letter O

TRACE the uppercase letter O.
Start at the green arrow.

1

O

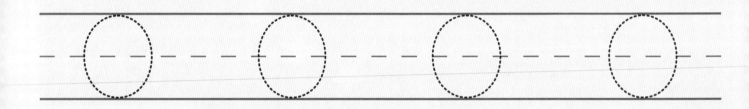

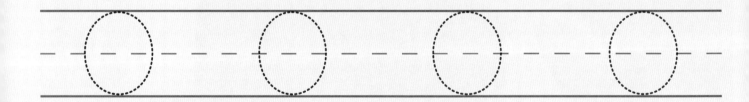

Now WRITE three uppercase Os.

1   2   3

Practice the Letter o

TRACE the lowercase letter o.
Start at the green arrow.

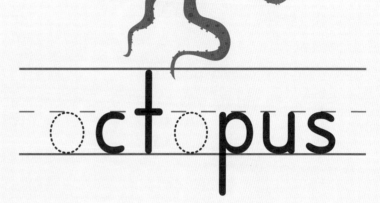

o c t o p u s

Now WRITE three lowercase **o**s.

The Letter Oo

Maze Crazy!

DRAW a line through the path marked with O and o to get to the owl.
Start at the blue arrow.

Cross Out

CROSS OUT the pictures that **don't** start with O.

The Letter Pp

Practice the Letter P

TRACE the uppercase letter **P**.
Start at the green arrow.

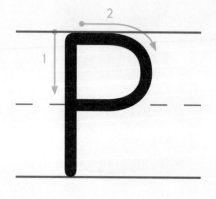

P

Pig

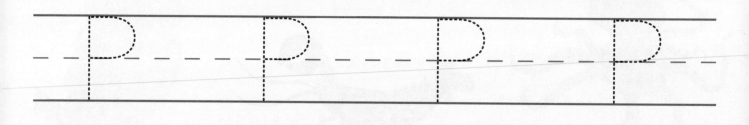

P P P P

P P P P

Now WRITE three uppercase **P**s.

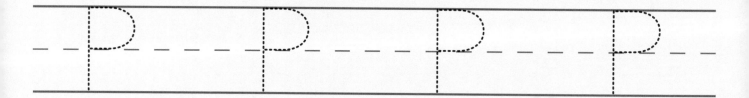

P

1   2   3

Practice the Letter p

TRACE the lowercase letter **p**.
Start at the green arrow.

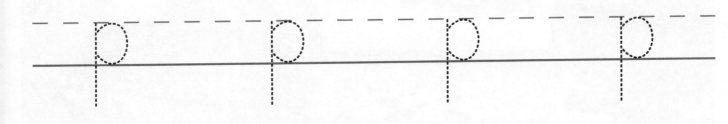

popcorn

Now WRITE three lowercase **p**s.

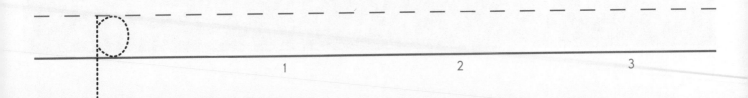

1   2   3

The Letter Pp

Hide and Seek

CIRCLE the things in the picture that start with **P**.

64

Finish the Word

FILL IN the blanks with **p** to finish the words. The letter may be at the beginning, middle, or end of the word.

1
izza

2

enguin

3
um kin

4
gra es

5
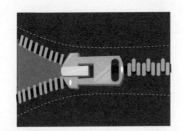
zi er

6

mo

Practice the Letter Q

TRACE the uppercase letter **Q**.
Start at the green arrow.

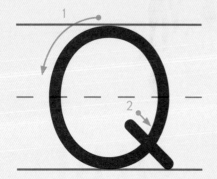

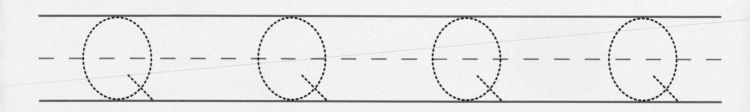

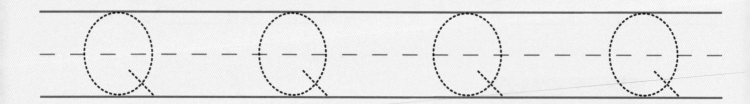

Now WRITE three uppercase **Q**s.

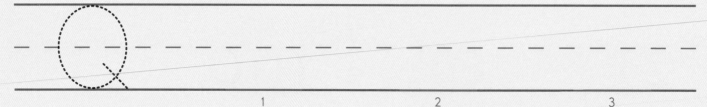

1   2   3

Practice the Letter q

TRACE the lowercase letter **q**.
Start at the green arrow.

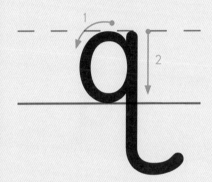

quilt

Now WRITE three lowercase **q**s.

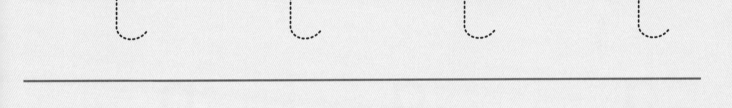

1   2   3

The Letter Qq

Match the Letters

FIND the lowercase **q**. DRAW a line from the uppercase **Q** to the lowercase **q**.

Q

y   t   p   q

Now COLOR the queens who are wearing lowercase **q**s.

Alphabet Art

COLOR the spaces that show **Q** or **q**.

Practice the Letter R

TRACE the uppercase letter R.
Start at the green arrow.

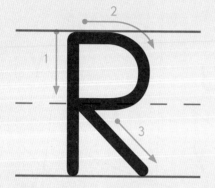

Now WRITE three uppercase **R**s.

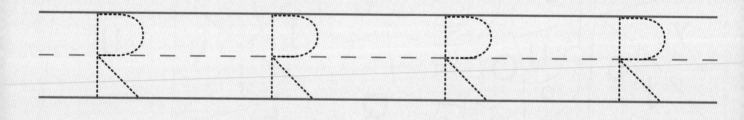

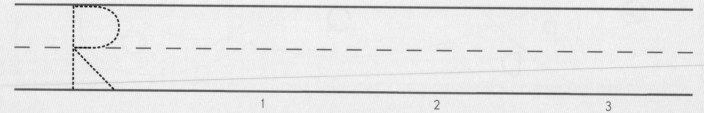

1   2   3

Practice the Letter r

TRACE the lowercase letter r.
Start at the green arrow.

rooster

Now WRITE three lowercase rs.

1   2   3

The Letter Rr

Cross Out

CROSS OUT the pictures that **don't** start with R.

Maze Crazy!

DRAW a line through the path marked with **R** and **r** to get to the rose.
Start at the yellow arrow.

Practice the Letter S

TRACE the uppercase letter S.
Start at the green arrow.

1

S

Sun

S   S   S   S

S   S   S   S

Now WRITE three uppercase Ss.

S

1   2   3

Practice the Letter s

TRACE the lowercase letter **s**.
Start at the green arrow.

s

scissors

s s s s

s s s s

Now WRITE three lowercase **s**s.

s

1   2   3

The Letter Ss

Finish the Word

FILL IN the blanks with **s** to finish the words. The letter may be at the beginning, middle, or end of the word.

1
_____ nowman

2

_____ even

3
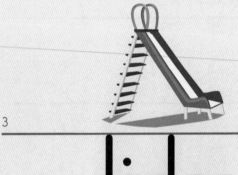
_____ lide

4
ne _____ t

5

dre _____

6
gla _____ e

Hide and Seek

CIRCLE the things in the picture that start with S.

The Letter Tt

Practice the Letter T

TRACE the uppercase letter T.
Start at the green arrow.

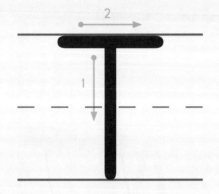

Turkey

Now WRITE three uppercase Ts.

1   2   3

Practice the Letter t

TRACE the lowercase letter **t**.
Start at the green arrow.

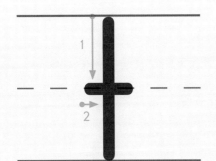

oo hbrush

Now WRITE three lowercase **t**s.

1   2   3

Match the Letters

FIND the lowercase t. DRAW a line from the uppercase T to the lowercase t.

T

j   l   f   t

Now COLOR the turkeys that are wearing lowercase ts.

Letter Draw

DRAW five things that start with T.

Tt

The Letter Uu

Practice the Letter U

TRACE the uppercase letter **U**.
Start at the green arrow.

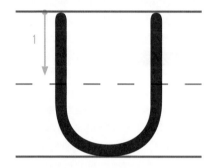

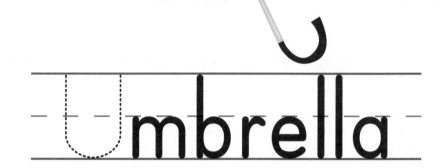

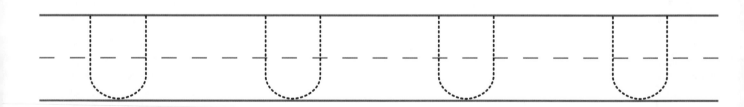

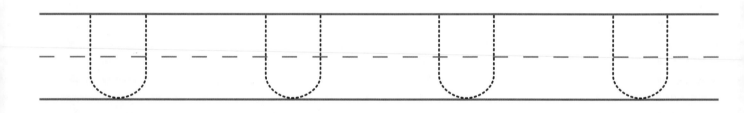

Now WRITE three uppercase **U**s.

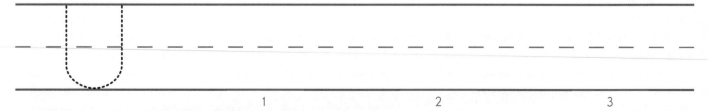

1   2   3

Practice the Letter u

TRACE the lowercase letter **u**.
Start at the green arrow.

underwear

Now WRITE three lowercase **u**s.

1   2   3

The Letter Uu

Cross Out

CROSS OUT the pictures that **don't** start with U.

Maze Crazy!

DRAW a line through the path marked with **U** and **u** to get to the underwear. Start at the blue arrow.

The Letter Vv

Practice the Letter V

TRACE the uppercase letter V.
Start at the green arrow.

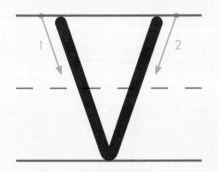

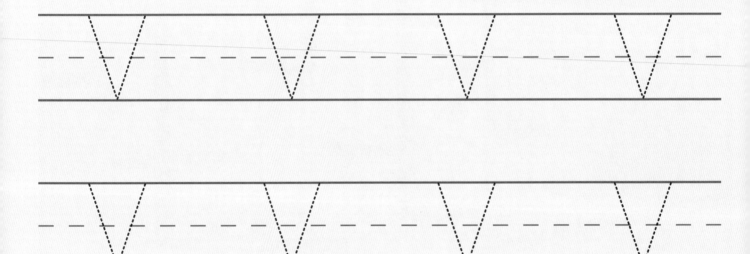

Van

Now WRITE three uppercase Vs.

1   2   3

Practice the Letter v

TRACE the lowercase letter v.
Start at the green arrow.

1   2

violin

Now WRITE three lowercase vs.

1   2   3

The Letter Vv

Finish the Word

FILL IN the blanks with **v** to finish the words. The letter may be at the beginning or middle of the word.

1
_egetables

2
oli_e

3
_ase

4
en_elope

5
se_en

6
_acuum

Alphabet Art

COLOR the spaces that show V or v.

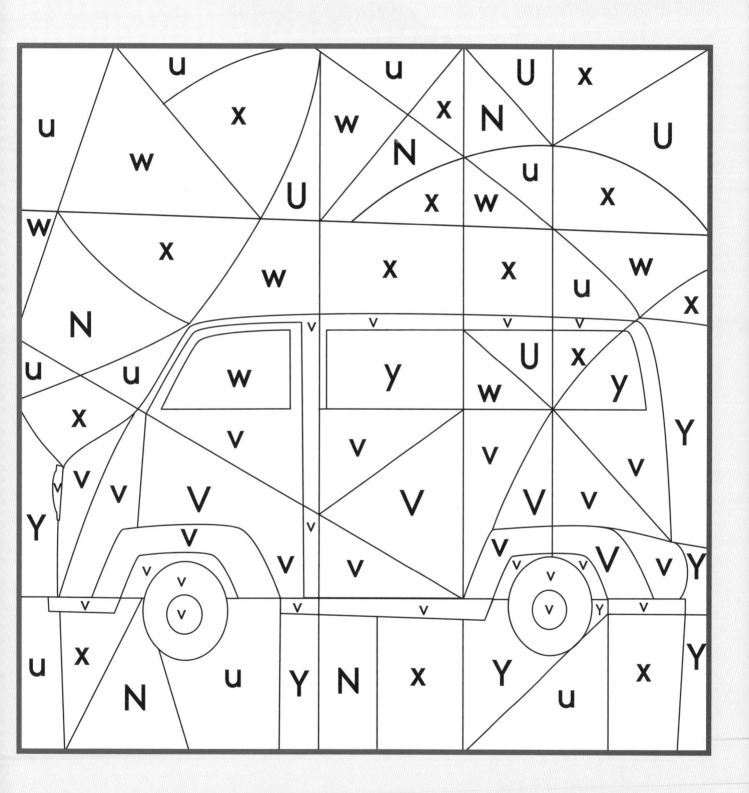

Practice the Letter W

TRACE the uppercase letter W.
Start at the green arrow.

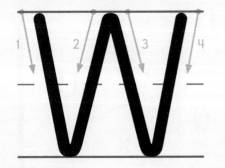

Whale

Now WRITE three uppercase **W**s.

1   2   3

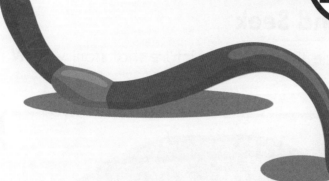

Practice the Letter w

TRACE the lowercase letter **w**.
Start at the green arrow.

worm

W   W   W   W

W   W   W   W

Now WRITE three lowercase **w**s.

W

1   2   3

The Letter Ww

Hide and Seek

CIRCLE the things in the picture that start with **W**.

Match the Letters

FILL IN the blanks with the matching lowercase letter.

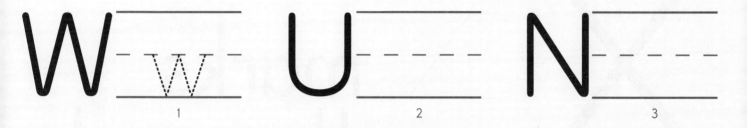

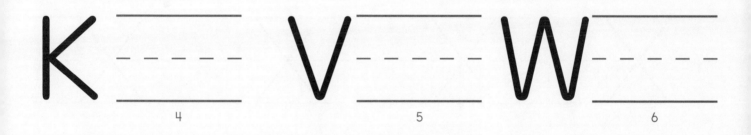

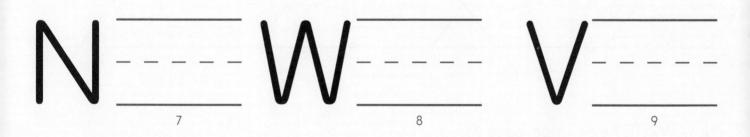

The Letter Xx

Practice the Letter X

TRACE the uppercase letter **X**.
Start at the green arrow.

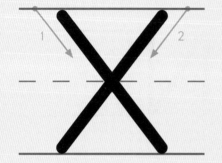

X marks the spot

Now WRITE three uppercase **X**s.

1   2   3

Practice the Letter x

TRACE the lowercase letter **x**.
Start at the green arrow.

x-ray

Now WRITE three lowercase **x**s.

1   2   3

The Letter Xx

Finish the Word

FILL IN the blanks with **x** to finish the words. The letter is at the end of these words.

1 ____
a

2 ____
si

3 ____
fo

Now COLOR the foxes that are wearing lowercase **x**s.

Maze Crazy!

DRAW a line through the path marked with **X** and **x** to get to X marks the spot.
Start at the yellow arrow.

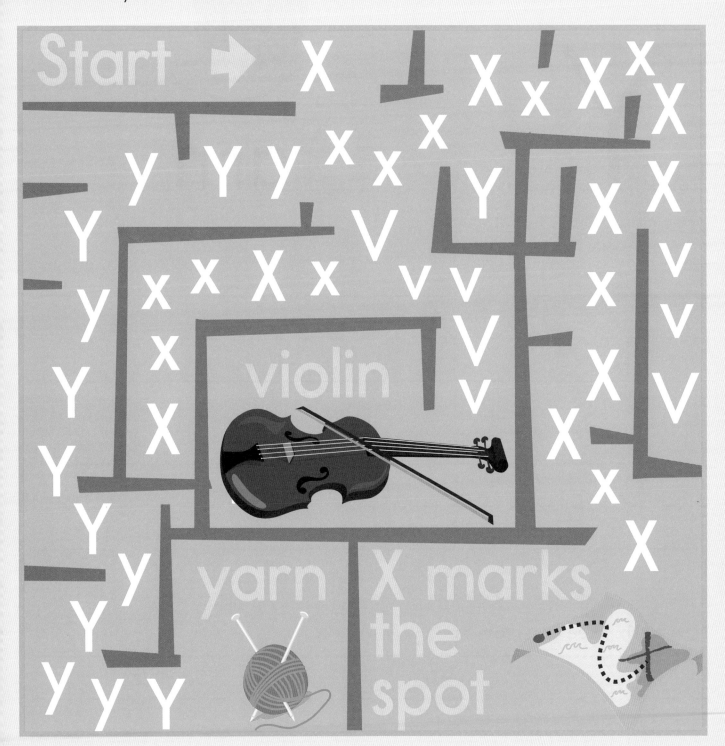

The Letter Yy

Practice the Letter Y

TRACE the uppercase letter Y.
Start at the green arrow.

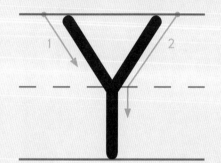

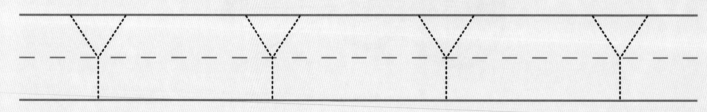

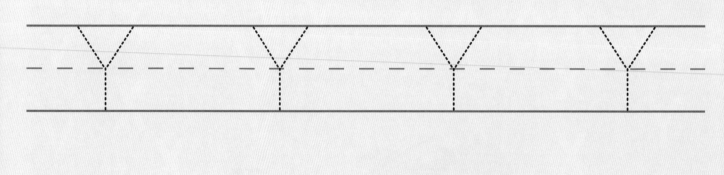

Now WRITE three uppercase Ys.

1   2   3

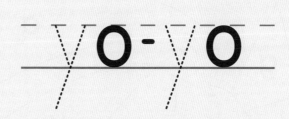

Practice the Letter y

TRACE the lowercase letter y.
Start at the green arrow.

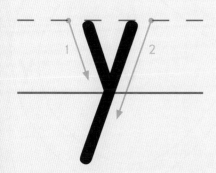

y o - y o

y   y   y   y

y   y   y   y

Now WRITE three lowercase ys.

y   1   2   3

The Letter Yy

Alphabet Art

COLOR the spaces that show Y or y.

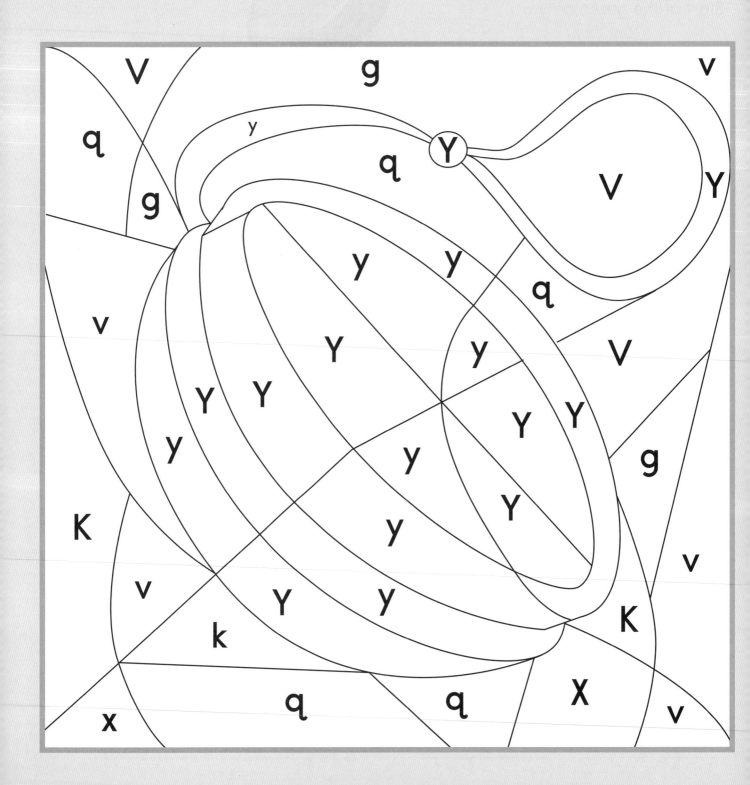

Finish the Word

FILL IN the blanks with y to finish the words. The letter may be at the beginning, middle, or end of the word.

1
_ellow

2
_arn

3
o-_o

4
lad_bug

5
ke_

6
fl_

Practice the Letter Z

TRACE the uppercase letter **Z**.
Start at the green arrow.

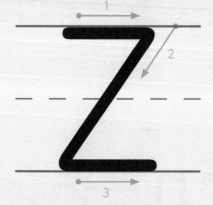

Zebra

Now WRITE three uppercase **Z**s.

1   2   3

Practice the Letter z

TRACE the lowercase letter **z**.
Start at the green arrow.

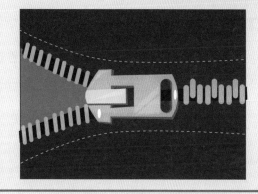

z̲i̲p̲p̲e̲r̲

Now WRITE three lowercase **z**s.

1   2   3

The Letter Zz

Maze Crazy!

DRAW a line through the path marked with **Z** and **z** to get to the zebra. Start at the blue arrow.

Finish the Word

FILL IN the blanks with **z** to finish the words. The letter may be at the beginning or middle of the word.

1

____ ebra

2

____ ipper

3

____ oo

4

____ ero

5

pi ____ ____ a

6

____ ig ____ ag

Answers

Page 4

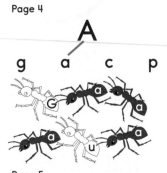

Page 5

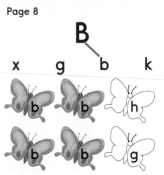

Page 8

Page 9
books, bull, boy, bread, bandage, bed, bucket, basketball, boots, bulldozer, bat

Page 12
Suggestions: cookie, castle, cup, candy, cat, caterpillar, cake, car, cow, cupcake, cap, carrot, crab, crayon, camera, clock, clown, coat, computer, crocodile, crown

Page 13

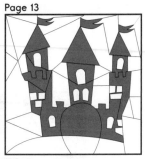

Page 16
door, doorknob, drum, dolphin, doll, dancer, dragon, dog, dress, dad, daughter

Page 17
1. dress, 2. duck, 3. dragon, 4. hand, 5. red, 6. candy

Page 20

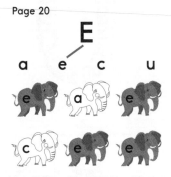

Page 21

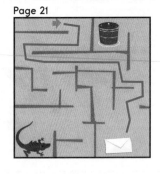

Page 24

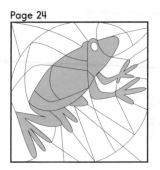

Page 25

Page 28
1. grapes, 2. guitar, 3. gift, 4. dog, 5. finger, 6. alligator

Page 29

Page 32

Page 33

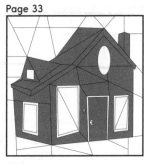

Page 36

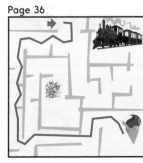

Page 37

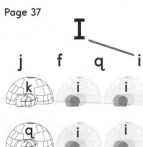

Page 40
jar, jellybeans, jump rope, jellyfish, juice box, jam, jacket

Page 41
1. juice, 2. jacket, 3. jet, 4. jellyfish, 5. jump rope, 6. jar

Page 44
1. kitten, 2. king, 3. kangaroo, 4. turkey, 5. monkey, 6. duck

Page 45

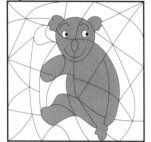

Page 48

Page 49

Page 52
Suggestions: mouse, money, monkey, monster, mug, milk, mitten, moon, man, mop, mat, maze, mushroom, mother, moose, mailbox, map, mouth

Page 53
1. mailbox, 2. mouse, 3. milk
4. snowman, 5. hammer, 6. worm

Page 56
1. nail, 2. king, 3. nest, 4. nine,
5. unicorn, 6. yarn

Page 57
nine, nest, necklace, net, newspaper, night, nightgown

Page 60

Page 61

Page 64
peas, pumpkin, peanuts, potatoes, pineapple, pots, pizza, pirate, pencil, pad, parrot, police officer, pepperoni

Page 65
1. pizza, 2. penguin, 3. pumpkin
4. grapes, 5. zipper, 6. mop

Page 68

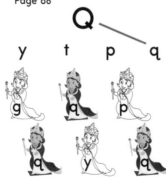

Page 69

Page 72

Page 73

Page 76
1. snowman, 2. seven, 3. slide
4. nest, 5. dress, 6. glasses

Page 77
sun, sky, swimmer, slide, sliding, swing, swinging, strawberries, spoon, soccer ball, sandwich, shovel, sand, sand castle, starfish, smiley face, swimsuit

Page 80

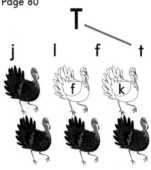

Page 81
Suggestions: turtle, teeth, toys, truck, tray, tomato, table, ten, telephone, toaster, toast, top, tent, tub, toilet, toes, tummy, tennis, towel, teddy bear, turkey, toothbrush, train, tree, ticket, taxi, triangle, tail, tiger, tractor

Page 84

Page 85

Page 88
1. vegetables, 2. olive, 3. vase,
4. envelope, 5. seven, 6. vacuum

Answers

Page 89

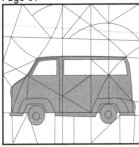

Page 92

whale, wave, watch, window, walrus, whistle, water, watermelon

Page 93

1. w, 2. u, 3. n, 4. k, 5. v, 6. w, 7. n, 8. w, 9. v

Page 96

1. ax, 2. six, 3. fox

Page 97

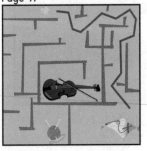

Page 100

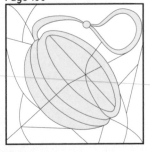

Page 101

1. yellow, 2. yarn, 3. yo-yo, 4. ladybug, 5. key, 6. fly

Page 104

Page 105

1. zebra, 2. zipper, 3. zoo, 4. zero, 5. pizza, 6. zigzag

Kindergarten
Reading Readiness

Alphabet Zone

Alphabet Letter Search

The alphabet letters are playing hide and seek. CIRCLE each letter when you find it in the picture.

Ⓐ B C D E F G H I J K L M N O P Q R S T U V W X Y Z

Alphabet Maze

FOLLOW the path marked with **lowercase** letters to help the bunny go home.

Complete the Alphabet

FILL IN the chart with the missing letters.

Mm   Ww   Ss   Bb   Ff

Aa ___1___ Cc Dd Ee

___2___ Gg Hh Ii Jj Kk

Ll ___3___ Nn Oo Pp

Qq Rr ___4___ Tt Uu

Vv ___5___ Xx Yy Zz

Match the Letters

DRAW a line to connect the uppercase and lowercase letters that go together.

A   k

T   e

D   d

K   a

E   t

What's My Sound?

CIRCLE the pictures with the **m** sound.
COLOR the pictures for fun.

Ss

What's My Sound?

DRAW lines from the "Ss" to pictures with the **s** sound. COLOR the pictures for fun.

Ff

Hide and Seek

LOOK at the farm. CIRCLE things that start with the **f** sound.

L l

2

What's My Sound?

CIRCLE the pictures with the l sound.
COLOR the pictures for fun.

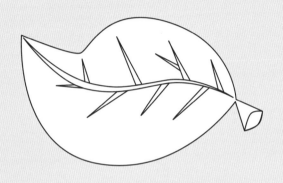
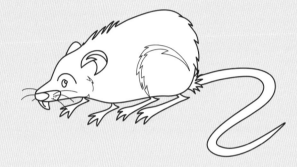
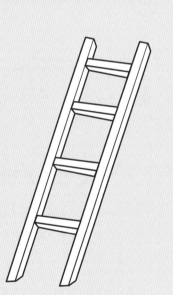

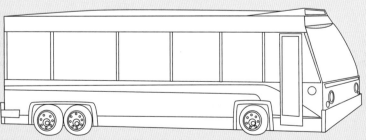

What's My Sound?

DRAW lines from the "Rr" to pictures with the **r** sound.
COLOR the pictures for fun.

Rr

Rr

T t

Draw It

LOOK at the train. DRAW your own pictures with the **t** sound on the blank train cars.

Hide and Seek

Look at the park. CIRCLE the things and activities
in the park that start with the **p** sound.

Pp

Nn

What's My Sound?

DRAW lines from the "Nn" to pictures that start with the **n** sound. COLOR the pictures for fun.

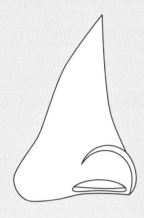

Nn

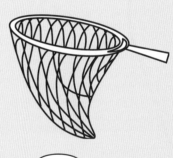

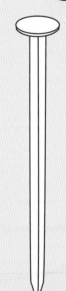

Bb

Draw It

LOOK at the big bag. DRAW your own pictures with the **b** sound inside the big bag.

C c

What's My Sound?

DRAW lines from the "Cc" to pictures with the **c** sound. COLOR the pictures for fun.

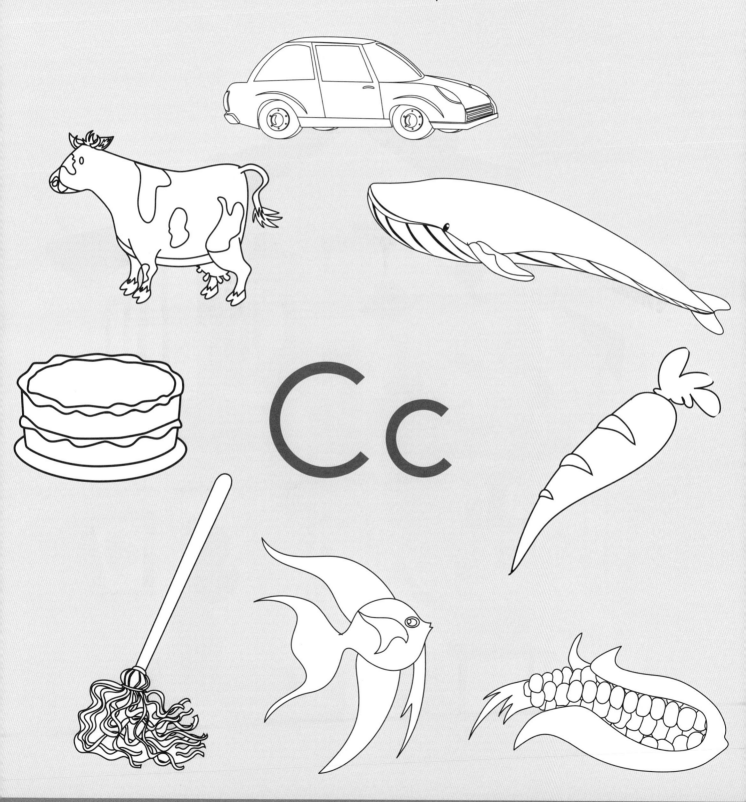

C c

Consonant Sounds

Hide and Seek

LOOK at the house. CIRCLE the things and activities in the house that start with the **h** sound.

Hh

Gg

What's My Sound?

CIRCLE the pictures with the **g** sound.
COLOR the pictures for fun.

Ww

What's My Sound?

DRAW lines from the "Ww" to pictures that start with the **w** sound. COLOR the pictures for fun.

V v

What's My Sound?

CIRCLE the pictures that start with the **v** sound.
COLOR the pictures for fun.

What's My Sound?

CIRCLE the pictures that start with the **d** sound.
COLOR the pictures for fun.

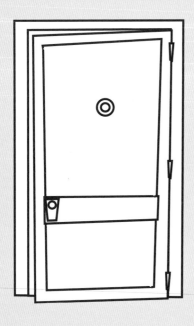

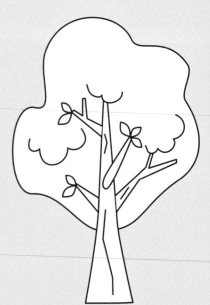

J j

What's My Sound?

DRAW lines from the "Jj" to pictures with the j sound. COLOR the pictures for fun.

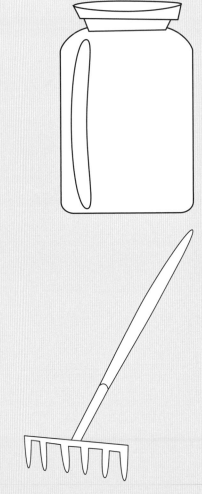

J j

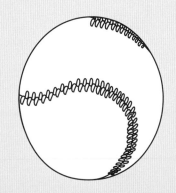

What's My Sound?

DRAW lines from the "Kk" to pictures that start with the **k** sound.
COLOR the pictures for fun.

Kk

Xx

Draw It

LOOK at the box. DRAW your own pictures with the **x** sound inside the box.

NOTE: Words that contain the sound but not the letter, such as **socks**, are okay.

What's My Sound?

CIRCLE the pictures that start with the y sound.
COLOR the pictures for fun.

Yy

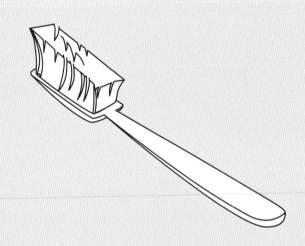

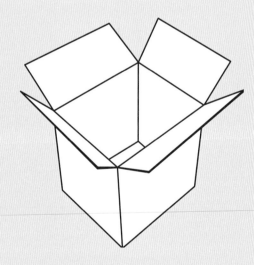

2

Zz

What's My Sound?

DRAW lines from the "Zz" to pictures that start with the **z** sound. COLOR the pictures for fun.

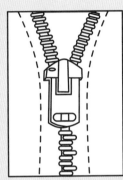

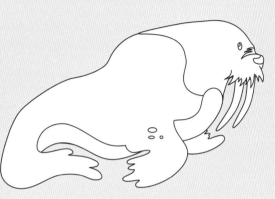

Zz

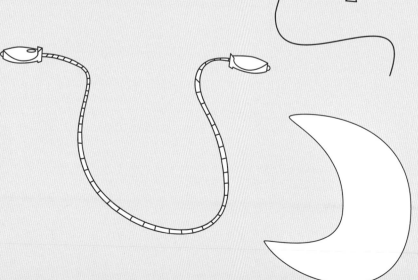

Consonant Sounds

What's My Sound?

DRAW lines from the "qu" to pictures with the **qu** sound.
COLOR the pictures for fun.

qu

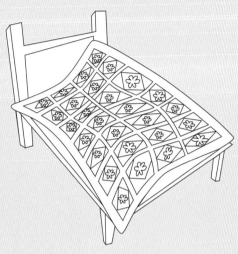

qu

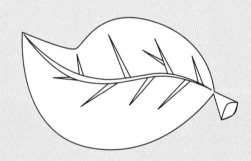

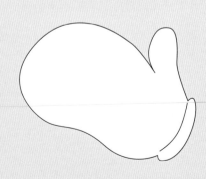

ck

What's My Sound?

DRAW lines from the "ck" to pictures with the **ck** sound. COLOR the pictures for fun.

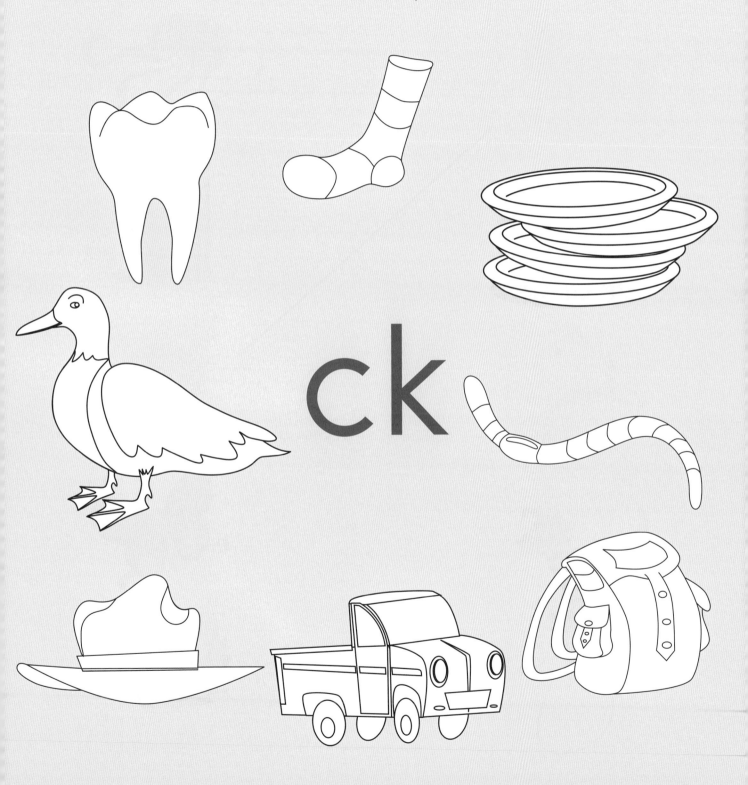

ck

Beginning Sounds

Match Up

LOOK at the pictures. DRAW a line between the pictures that **begin** with the same sound.

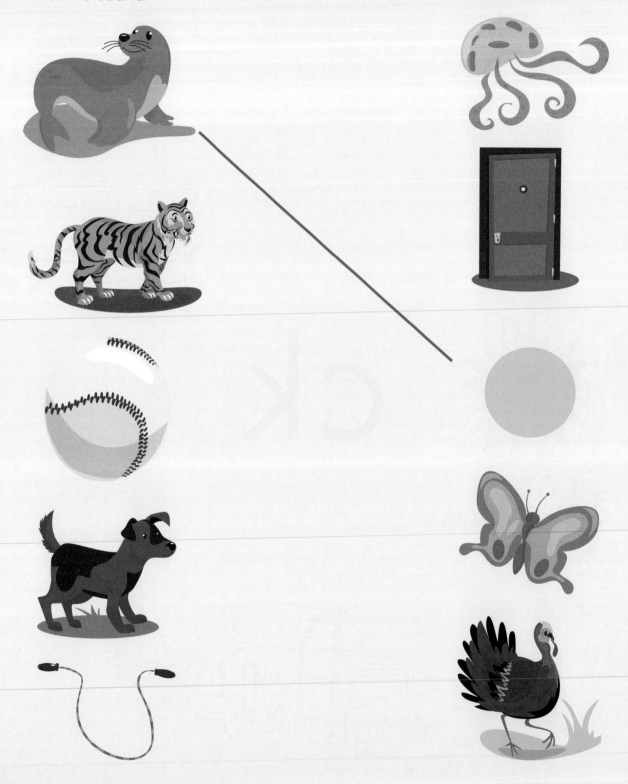

Let's do some more!

Circle It

LOOK at the letter. CIRCLE the picture in the row that **begins** with the letter sound.

Hh

Nn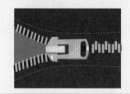

Rr

Ww

3

Starting Line

LOOK at the picture. WRITE the letter that makes the sound at the **beginning** of the word.

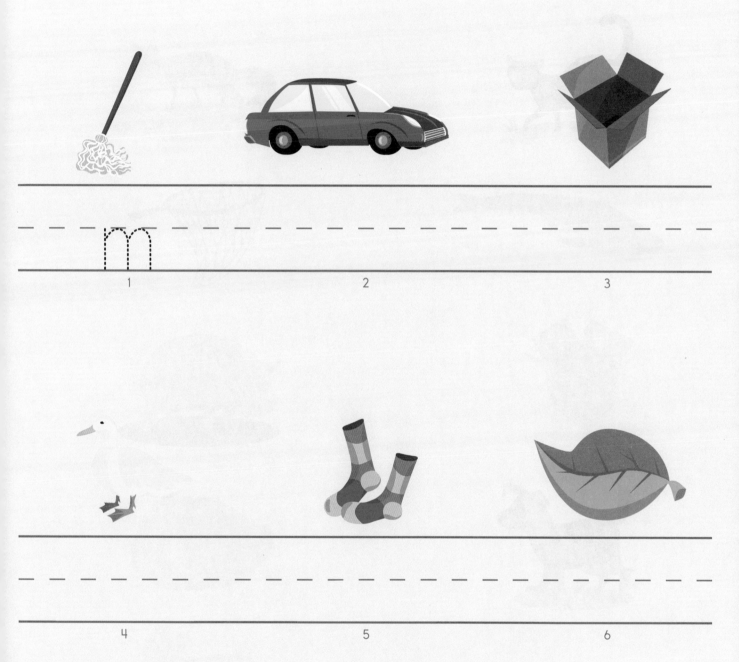

1

2

3

4

5

6

Ending Sounds

Match Up

LOOK at the pictures. DRAW a line between the pictures that **end** with the same sound.

Let's do some more!

Ending Sounds

Circle It

LOOK at the letter. CIRCLE the picture in the row that **ends** with the letter sound.

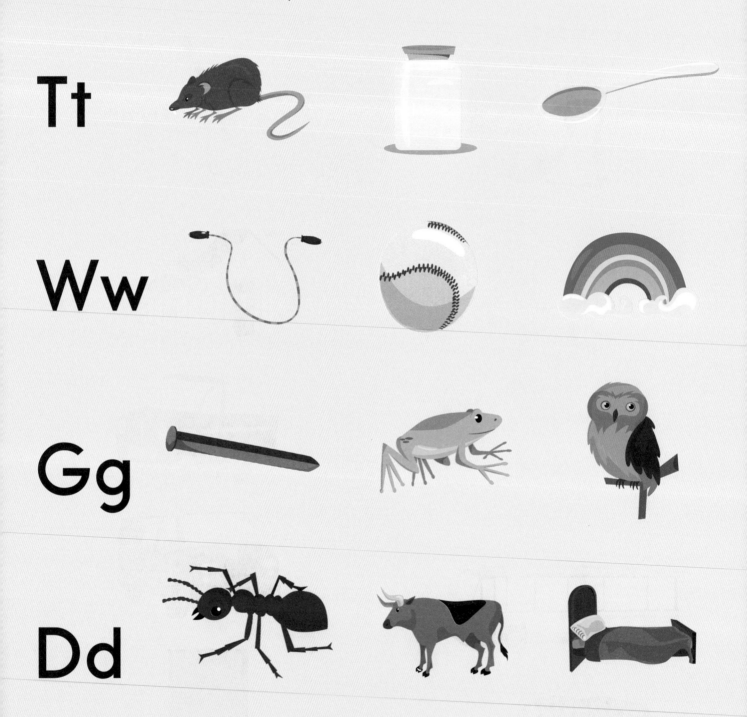

Finish Line

LOOK at the picture. WRITE the letter that makes the sound at the **end** of the word.

_____

- -

_____

1   2   3

_____

- -

_____

4   5   6

Short Vowels

What's My Sound?

DRAW lines from the "a" to pictures with the short **a** sound.
COLOR the pictures for fun.

a

a

What Am I?

MATCH the pictures to the words.

hat

pan

rat

bag

cat

Short Vowels

What's My Sound?

DRAW lines from the "e" to pictures with the short **e** sound.
COLOR the pictures for fun.

146

What Am I?

MATCH the pictures to the words.

web

hen

ten

net

bed

Short Vowels

What's My Sound?

DRAW lines from the "i" to pictures with the short i sound.
COLOR the pictures for fun.

What Am I?

MATCH the pictures to the words.

kick

bib

pig

sit

kid

What's My Sound?

DRAW lines from the "o" to pictures with the short **o** sound.
COLOR the pictures for fun.

What Am I?

MATCH the pictures to the words.

rod

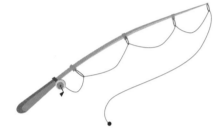

pot

top

mop

box

What's My Sound?

DRAW lines from the "u" to pictures with the short **u** sound.
COLOR the pictures for fun.

U

u

What Am I?

MATCH the pictures to the words.

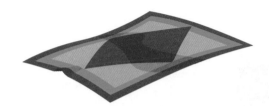
cup

tub

mud

bug

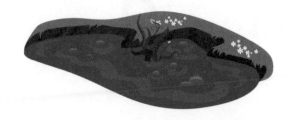
rug

Let's Rhyme

Time to Rhyme

FILL IN the missing letter to make a rhyme to match the picture.

1

f   t   c   t

2

b   g   h   g

Match Up

MATCH the pictures that sound alike.

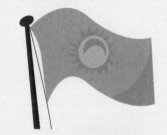

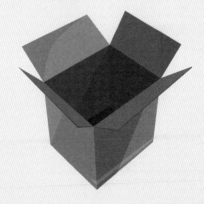

Let's Rhyme

Time to Rhyme

FILL IN the missing letter to make a rhyme to match the picture.

1 _____

m   n   r   n

2 _____

f   n   r   n

Match Up

MATCH the pictures that sound alike.

Time to Rhyme

FILL IN the missing letter to make a rhyme that matches the picture.

1   b   g   d   g

2   p   p   c   p

Match Up

MATCH the pictures that sound alike.

Time to Read

READ each sentence out loud. MATCH the sentences to the pictures.

I see the hat.

1. I see a man.

2. I see the rat.

3. I see a hen.

4. I see the bed.

7

Make a Book

DRAW a picture to match each sentence.

My Very Own Book
What Do I See?
Pictures by

_____

2

I see a cat.

4

I see a pan.

6

I see a jet.

8

I see a ham.

10

I see a bag.

Turn the page to finish your book.

Finish Your Book

CUT on the dotted lines. ASK a parent to staple the pages together. READ your book out loud. ✂

3

I see the hat.

1

I see the map.

7

I see the van.

5

I see the net.

11

I see the jam.

9

I see a bat.

Find the Missing Word

LOOK at each sentence. LOOK at the words in the word box. WRITE the correct word in each blank. CROSS OUT the words as you use them.

I	a	~~see~~	jet

1. I _see_ the rat.

2. _____ see a man.

3. I see a _____.

4. I see _____ bed.

Time to Read

READ each sentence out loud. MATCH the sentences to the pictures.

1. I see a man and a cat.

2. The pig is wet.

3. I see a fox in a hat.

4. The rat is in the box.

Make a Book

DRAW a picture to match each sentence.

My Very Own Book
What Do I See?
Pictures by

_____

2

I see a man in a jet.

4

The ham is in the pan.

6

The cat is in the bed.

8

It is a big top.

10

It is a red dot.

Turn the page to finish your book.

More Words to Know

Finish Your Book

CUT on the dotted lines. ASK a parent to staple the pages together. READ your book out loud. ✂

3

I see a pig in a pen.

1

I see a kid and a pet.

7

The dog is in the van.

5

The rat is in the log.

11

It is a wet mop.

9

It is a hot pot.

Find the Missing Word

LOOK at each sentence. LOOK at the words in the word box. WRITE the correct word in each blank. CROSS OUT the words as you use them.

It	in	is	and

1. I see a cat _____ a dog.

2. The fox _____ red.

3. _____ is a big net.

4. The fan is _____ the den.

Up and Down

Circle It

LOOK at the word. CIRCLE the picture that matches the word.

 **up** 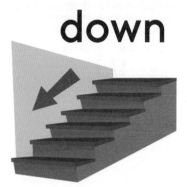 **down**

1. up

2. up

3. down

4. down

Which Way?

WRITE the word "up" or "down" to match the picture.

1. The jet is _____.

2. The man is _____.

3. The jet is _____.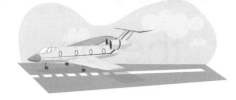

4. The man is _____.

Time to Read

MATCH the sentences to the pictures. READ each sentence out loud.

1. Mom said,
   "Go to bed."

2. The van can
   go up.

3. I see you in
   the bus.

4. Liz said "sit"
   to the dog.

Make a Book

DRAW a picture to match each sentence.

My Very Own Book

The Story of Nan and Pat

Pictures by

_____

2

Pat had a rat.

4

Pat saw Nan.

6

Nan said, "Yes, you can pet the dog."

8

Pat said, "Yes, you can pet the rat."

10

Nan pet the rat.

Turn the page to finish your book.

Finish Your Book

CUT on the dotted lines. ASK a parent to staple the pages together. READ your book out loud. ✂

3

Nan saw Pat.

1

Nan had a dog.

7

Nan said, "Can I pet the rat?"

5

Pat said, "Can I pet the dog?"

11

The dog and the rat had a nap.

9

Pat pet the dog.

Find the Missing Word

LOOK at each sentence. LOOK at the words in the word box. WRITE the correct word in each blank. CROSS OUT the words as you use them.

said	go	to	down

1. You _____ up in the jet.

2. I sit _____ in the jet.

3. You _____, "It is fun."

4. The dog ran _____ the man.

Colors

Time to Read

LOOK at the color word. CIRCLE the picture that matches the color.

red   green   blue   yellow

1. red

2. green

3. blue

4. yellow

Make a Book

DRAW a picture to match each sentence.

My Very Own Book

Red, Green, Blue, and Yellow

Pictures by

_____

2

The sack is blue.

4

The sun is yellow.

6

The bed is blue.

8

The bug is yellow.

10

The bus is yellow.

Turn the page to finish your book.

Finish Your Book

CUT on the dotted lines. ASK a parent to staple the pages together. READ your book out loud.

3

The cup is red.

1

The box is green.

7

The fox is red.

5

The sock is green.

11

The hat is red.

9

The jet is blue.

Draw It

READ each color word out loud. DRAW three things the same color inside each square.

yellow	red
blue	**green**

Big and Little

Circle It

LOOK at the word. CIRCLE the picture that matches the word.

big

little

1. big   

2. little      

3. big   

4. little   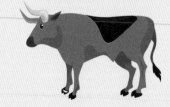

Blank Out

WRITE the word "big" or "little" to match the picture.

1. The van is _____.

2. The egg is _____.

3. The top is _____.

4. The bed is _____.

Match Up

READ each sentence out loud. MATCH the sentences to the pictures.

1. I have a green box.

2. I have a yellow box for you.

3. The rat is on the big rug.

4. We have a blue sack.

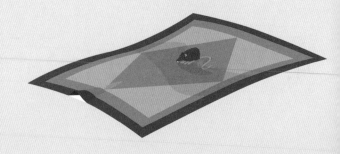

Make a Book

DRAW a picture to match each sentence.

My Very Own Book

A Dog, a Cat, and Hats

Pictures by

_____

2

We have a little cat.

4

The cat is on the rug.

6

We have a red hat for the cat.

8

We put the red hat on the cat.

10

We hug the cat.

Turn the page to finish your book.

Finish Your Book

CUT on the dotted lines. ASK a parent to staple the pages together. READ your book out loud. ✂

3

The dog is on the rug.

1

We have a big dog.

7

We put the blue hat on the dog.

5

We have a blue hat for the dog.

11

We have a dog and a cat in hats.

9

We hug the dog.

Find the Missing Word

LOOK at each sentence. LOOK at the words in the word box. WRITE the correct word in each blank. CROSS OUT the words as you use them.

for	have	on	We

1. We _____ a big van.

2. The mud is _____ the rug.

3. I have a job _____ you.

4. _____ see the yellow bus.

More Colors

Match Up

LOOK at the color word. CIRCLE the picture in the row that matches the color.

orange purple **black** **brown**

1. orange

2. purple

3. black

4. brown

Make a Book

DRAW a picture to match each sentence.

My Very Own Book

Colors

Pictures by

_____

2

The bat is black.

4

The log is brown.

6

The rock is brown.

8

The mud is brown.

10

The pan is black.

Turn the page to finish your book.

Finish Your Book

CUT on the dotted lines. ASK a parent to staple the pages together. READ your book out loud. ✂

3

The rug is purple.

1

The cat is orange.

7

The jam is purple.

5

The van is orange.

11

The hat is purple.

9

The yam is orange.

Draw It

READ each color word out loud. DRAW three things the same color inside each square.

orange	purple
black	**brown**

Story Characters

Who Is It?

The people and the animals in a story are the **characters**.

Animals

People

CIRCLE the pictures that can be characters in a story.

Who Is It?

READ the story out loud.

The Mud

The pig is in the mud. The dog is in the mud. The rat is in the mud. The hen is in the mud. The mud is brown. The mud is wet. It is fun.

CIRCLE the characters in the story.

Story Characters

Who Is It?

READ the story out loud.

> ### The Mat
>
> The duck ran to the man. The cat ran to the man. The duck sat on the mat. The cat sat on the mat. The man fed the duck and the cat on the mat.

CIRCLE the characters in the story.

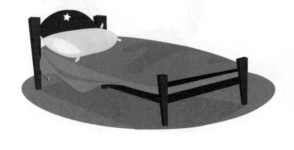

Who Is It?

READ the story out loud.

The Rat

A kid sat on a big rock. A dog sat on the rock. A cat sat on the rock. The kid said, "I see a rat." The cat ran. The dog ran. The kid ran.

DRAW the characters in the story.

Story Setting

Where Is It?

The place and time in a story create the **setting**.

Place

Time

CIRCLE the pictures that can be the setting for a story.

Where Is It?

READ the story out loud.

The Cat

I look for the cat. I look on the bed. The cat is not on the bed. I look on the rug. The cat is not on the rug. I look in a big box. I see the cat. It is in the big box.

CIRCLE the setting for the story.

Story Setting

Where Is It?

READ the story out loud.

> ### The Run
>
> He can run. She can run. I can run. You can run. We run to the rock. We run to the log. It is hot. We run in the sun.

CIRCLE the setting for the story.

Where Is It?

READ the story out loud.

The Van

Dad is in the van. I get in the van. You get in the van. We look at the map. We go up. We go down. We go and go in the van.

DRAW the setting for the story.

Story Sequence

What's the Order?

READ the story out loud.

Jam and Ham

I have a pot. I put ham in the pot. I put jam in the pot. I mix the ham and jam. Yum!

WRITE 1, 2, and 3 to show the beginning, middle, and end of the story.

___   ___   ___

What's the Order?

A story has a beginning, a middle, and an end.

LOOK at the pictures. WRITE 1, 2, and 3 to show the correct order.

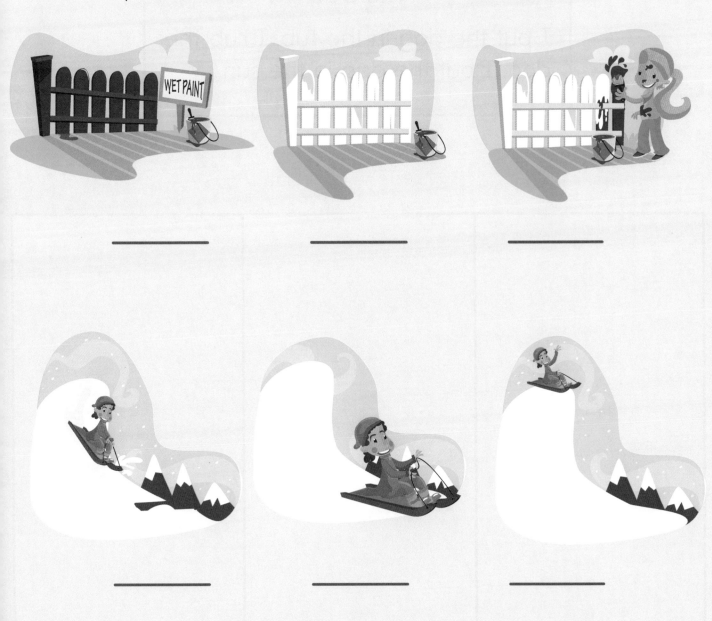

_____

_____

_____

_____

_____

_____

What's the Order?

READ the story out loud. DRAW the beginning, middle, and end of the story.

> ### The Dog
>
> I put the dog in the tub. I rub the dog. I put the dog in the sun.

1	2	3

What's the Order?

READ the story out loud. DRAW the beginning, middle, and end of the story.

The Cat Nap

I sit on the bed. I pat the cat.

I take a nap with the cat.

1	2	3

Story Problem and Solution

What's the Solution?

Most stories have a problem and a solution.

For example:

| Problem | Solution |

LOOK at the problem. DRAW the solution.

| Problem | Solution |

What's the Solution?

LOOK at the problem.

Problem

CIRCLE the correct solution to the problem.

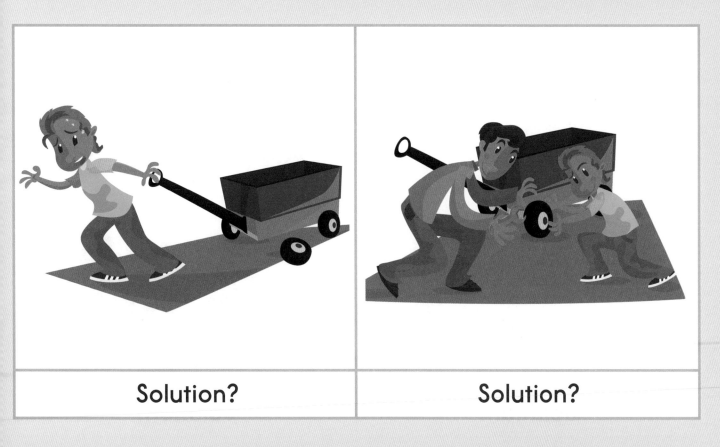

Solution?   Solution?

Story Problem and Solution

What's the Solution?

LOOK at the problem.

Problem

CIRCLE the correct solution to the problem.

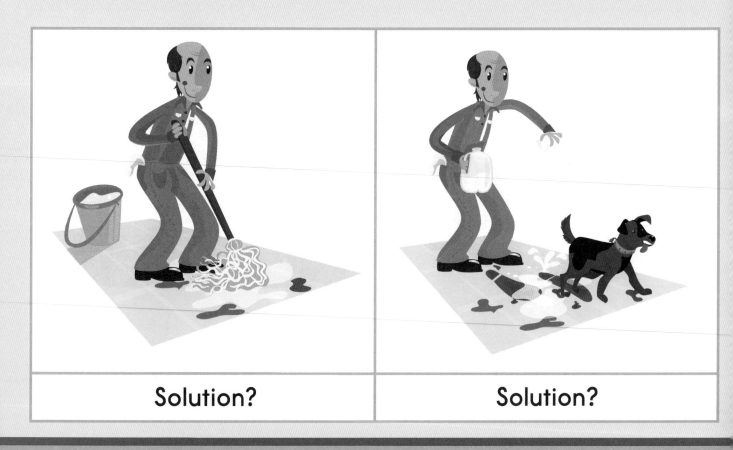

Solution?   Solution?

What's the Solution?

READ the story out loud.

Ben

Ben hid. I look in the den. Ben is not in the den. I look in the tub. I see Ben. He is in the tub.

DRAW the problem in the story. DRAW the solution in the story.

Problem	Solution

Answers

Page 110

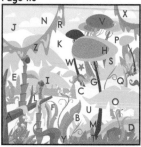

Page 111

Page 112

1. Bb 2. Ff 3. Mm 4. Ss 5. Ww

Page 113

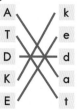

Page 114

mouse, moon, mitten, map, monkey

Page 115

sun, snail, stop, spoon, star

Page 116

fish, fence, frog, flies, flowers, farmer, face, fruit, flag, fan

Page 117

leaf, lightbulb, ladybug, ladder

Page 118

rainbow, rocket, robot, ring, rake

Page 119

Suggestions: tree, top, teeth, toothbrush, turkey, TV, table, toys, teacher, tea, tie, telephone

Page 120

police, play, path, picnic, pizza, piece of pizza, pie, purse, parrot, paint, painter, painting, person, puppy, post, picnic basket

Page 121

nose, net, nail, nine, nest

Page 122

Suggestions: bat, bug, boy, bread, butter, bottle, bone, bowl, button, bow, balloon, banana, belt

Page 123

car, carrot, corn, cake, cow

Page 124

ham, horse, hat, hang, hanger, hammer, heart, hair, hat stand, hands

Page 125

glasses, girl, goat, grapes

Page 126

whale, wagon, walrus, worm, window

Page 127

volcano, violin, van, vegetables

Page 128

door, dress, dishes, doll

Page 129

juice box, jar, jellyfish, jump rope

Page 130
kitten, kangaroo, kick, key

Page 131
Suggestions (can contain letter or sound): ox, taxi, fox, box, ax, six, rocks, socks, trucks, ducks, names with the x sound like Max or Rex

Page 132
yarn, yo-yo

Page 133
zebra, zipper, zoo

Page 134
quilt, question mark, queen

Page 135
sock, backpack, truck, duck

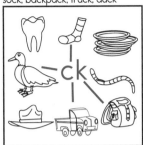

Page 136

Page 137

Page 138

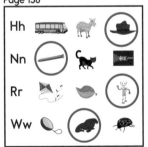

Page 139
1. m, 2. c (or k), 3. b, 4. d, 5. s, 6. l

Page 140

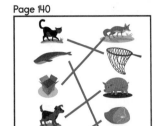

Page 141

Page 142

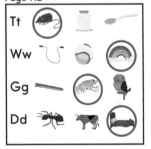

Page 143
1. n, 2. t, 3. l
4. m, 5. s, 6. g

Page 144
fan, map, rat, ham, bat

Page 145

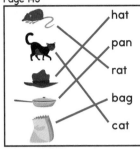
hat
pan
rat
bag
cat

Page 146
nest, net, egg, dress, bed

Page 147

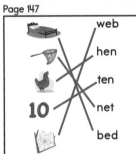
web
hen
ten
net
bed

Page 148
pig, zipper, fish, six, bib

Page 149

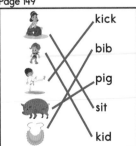
kick
bib
pig
sit
kid

Answers

Page 150
dog, lobster, mop, socks, box

Pages 151

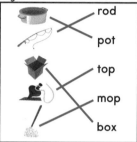

rod

pot

top

mop

box

Page 152
plug, drum, bus, duck, thumb

Page 153

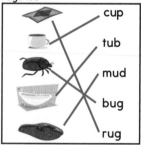

cup

tub

mud

bug

rug

Page 154
1. fat cat
2. bug hug

Page 155

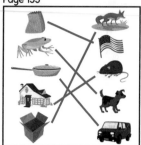

Page 156
1. man ran
2. fun run

Page 157

Page 158
1. big dig
2. pup cup

Page 159

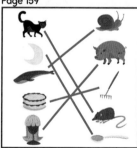

Page 160

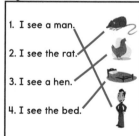

Pages 161–162
Each picture should match the sentence.

Page 163
1. I **see** the rat.
2. **I** see a man.
3. I see a **jet**.
4. I see **a** bed.

Page 164

1. I see a man and a cat.

2. The pig is wet.

3. It is a fox in a hat.

4. The rat is in the box.

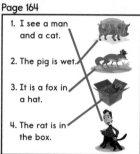

Pages 165–166
Each picture should match the sentence.

Page 167
1. I see a cat **and** a dog.
2. The fox **is** red.
3. **It** is a big net.
4. The fan is **in** the den.

Page 168

1. up

2. up

3. down

4. down

Page 169
1. The jet is **up**.
2. The man is **up**.
3. The jet is **down**.
4. The man is **down**.

Page 170

1. Mom said, "Go to bed."

2. The van can go up.

3. I see you in the bus.

4. Liz said "sit" to the dog.

Pages 171–172
Each picture should match the sentence.

Page 173
1. You **go** up in the jet.
2. I sit **down** in the jet.
3. You **said**, "It is fun."
4. The dog ran **to** the man.

Page 174

1. red

2. green

3. blue

4. yellow

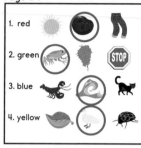

Pages 175–176
Each picture should match the sentence.

Page 177
Suggestions:
yellow: school bus, sun, duck
red: fire engine, stop sign, apple
blue: whale, water, blueberry
green: tree, leaf, dragon

Page 178

1. big

2. little

3. big

4. little

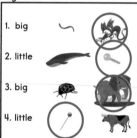

Page 179
1. The van is **big**.
2. The egg is **little**.
3. The top is **little**.
4. The bed is **big**.

Page 180

1. I have a green box.

2. I have a yellow box for you.

3. The rat is on the big rug.

4. We have a blue sack.

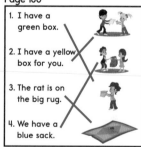

Pages 181–182
Each picture should match the sentence.

Page 183
1. We **have** a big van.
2. The mud is **on** the rug.
3. I have a job **for** you.
4. **We** see the yellow bus.

Answers

Page 184

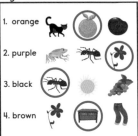

1. orange
2. purple
3. black
4. brown

Pages 185–186
Each picture should match the sentence.

Page 187
Suggestions:
orange: orange, goldfish
purple: flower, plum
black: ant, blackberry, road
brown: paper bag, mud, desk

Page 188
queen, cow, doctor, lion

Page 189
pig, dog, rat, hen

Page 190
man, cat, duck

Page 191
Pictures of a kid, a dog, a cat, and a rat

Page 192
house, barn, night

Page 193

Page 194

Page 195
Picture of a van on a road (on a hill)

Page 196

3   1   2

Page 197

3   1   2

2   3   1

Page 198
Pictures should match the story sequence.

Page 199
Pictures should match the story sequence.

Page 200
Picture should show a solution to the problem.

Page 201

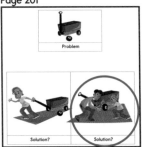

Problem

Solution?   Solution?

Page 202

Problem

Solution?   Solution?

Page 203
Pictures should match the story problem and solution.

Kindergarten
Beginning Word Games

X Marks the Spot

LOOK at the words in the word box. Can you find these things in the **winter** picture?
PUT an X over each one.

| snow | tree | owl | rock | fox | snowman |

Mystery Picture

FIND the spaces with the word **fall**. COLOR those spaces red to see the mystery picture.

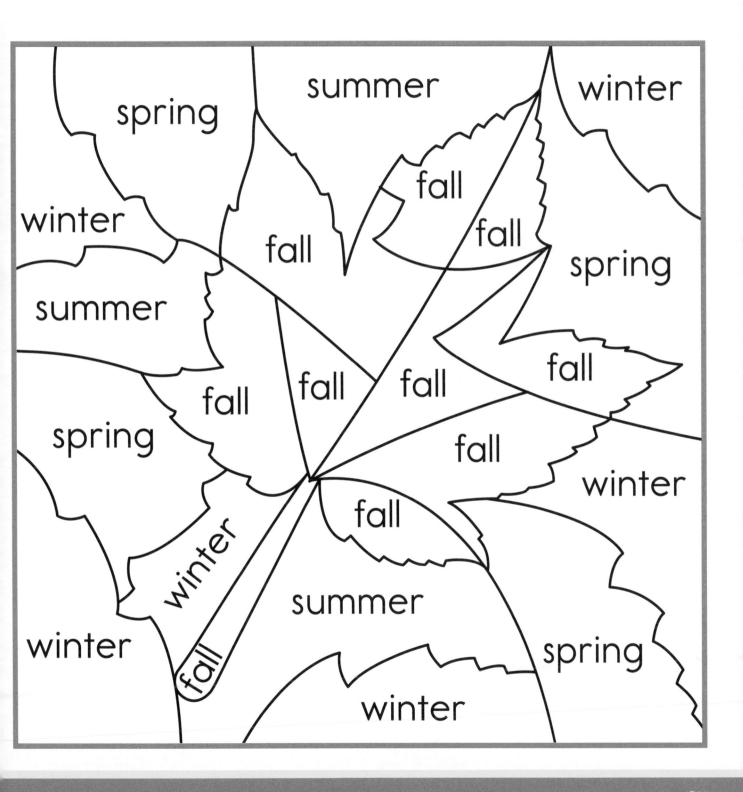

X Marks the Spot

LOOK at the words in the word box. Can you find these things in the **summer** picture?
PUT an X over each one.

sun	ant	ball	bird	grass	dog

Mystery Picture

FIND the spaces with the word **spring**. COLOR those spaces pink to see the mystery picture.

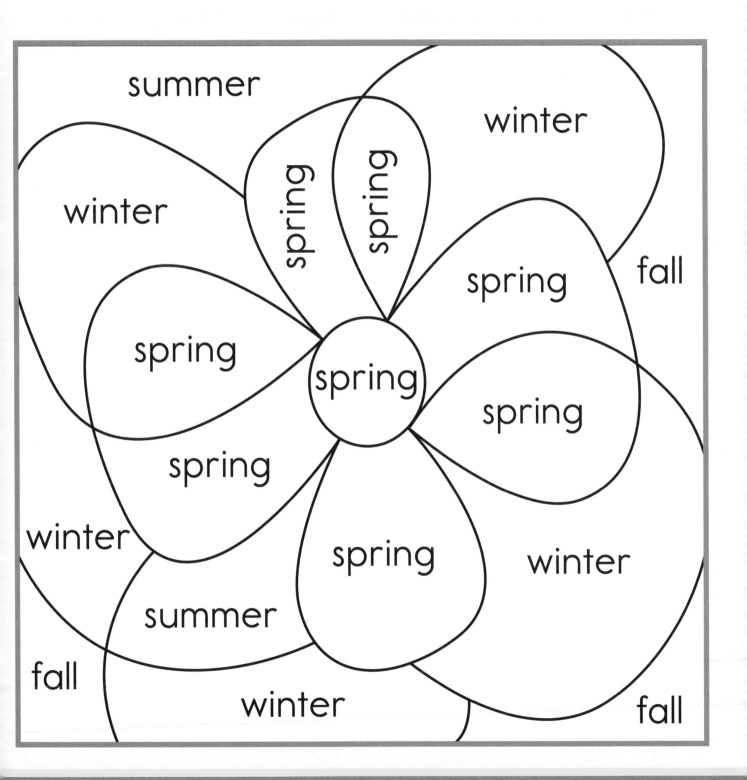

Word Endings

Word Hunt

CIRCLE the words in the grid that end in **-ad**.
Words go across and down.

sad	bad	dad	had	mad	pad

a	z	q	c	l	h	k
e	b	n	s	f	a	m
s	a	f	a	u	d	x
f	d	m	d	v	w	d
h	j	u	o	p	i	a
r	c	m	a	d	s	d
y	q	g	f	o	e	l
p	a	d	t	v	b	a

Pond Crossing

DRAW a line through the words that end in **-ad** to help the frog jump across the pond.

Start

mad

cat

rat

yam

ram

sad

ham

hat

jam

dam

pad

lad

mat

sat

dad

End

Word Hunt

-ag

CIRCLE the words in the grid that end in **-ag**.
Words go across and down.

bag	rag	sag	tag	wag

a	e	z	x	d	s	h
w	y	u	r	e	a	c
a	c	r	a	s	g	p
g	b	v	g	j	k	w
i	l	m	h	e	t	s
b	a	g	y	t	f	h
o	r	v	u	a	b	k
t	n	i	s	g	q	d

Find the Path

DRAW a line through the words that end in **-ag** to help the ant out of the anthill.

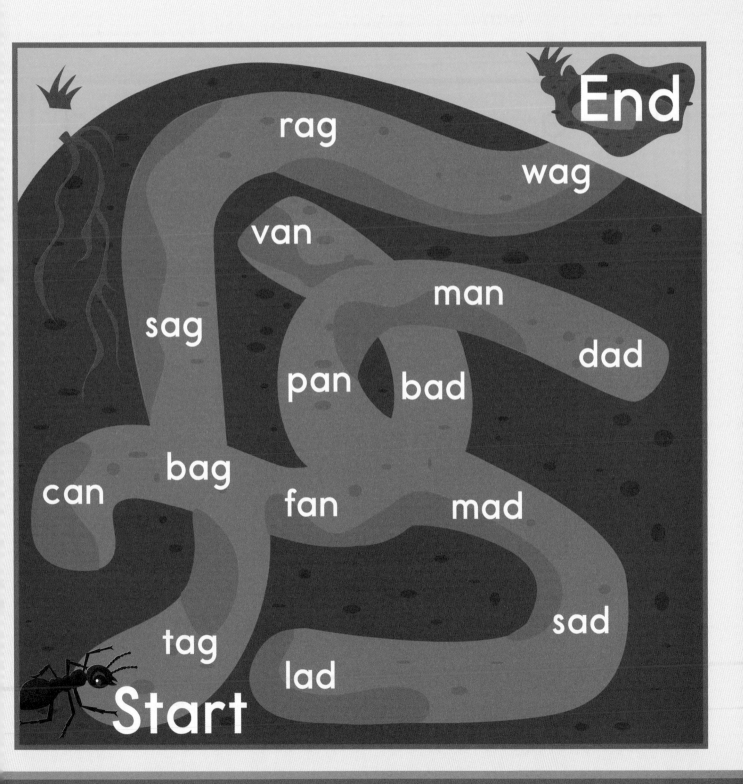

Word Hunt

-am

CIRCLE the words in the grid that end in **-am**.
Words go across or down.

| dam | ham | yam | ram | jam |

h	a	m	e	y	b	d
c	k	m	i	a	r	p
q	z	x	o	m	n	e
u	d	a	m	v	o	j
r	t	s	h	f	i	a
j	q	c	u	l	s	m
r	a	m	r	e	w	z
a	g	p	o	t	t	e

Find the Path

DRAW a line through the words that end in **-am** to help the ram down the mountain.

Start

rag

ram

nag

wag

bag

dam

fat

yam

tag

rat

mat

pat

jam

End

ham

hat

Rhyming Fun

Connect the Dots

DRAW a line to connect the words that sound like **mad**. Connect them in ABC order.

HINT: I sit in the sand under the sea. An ocean animal lives in me.

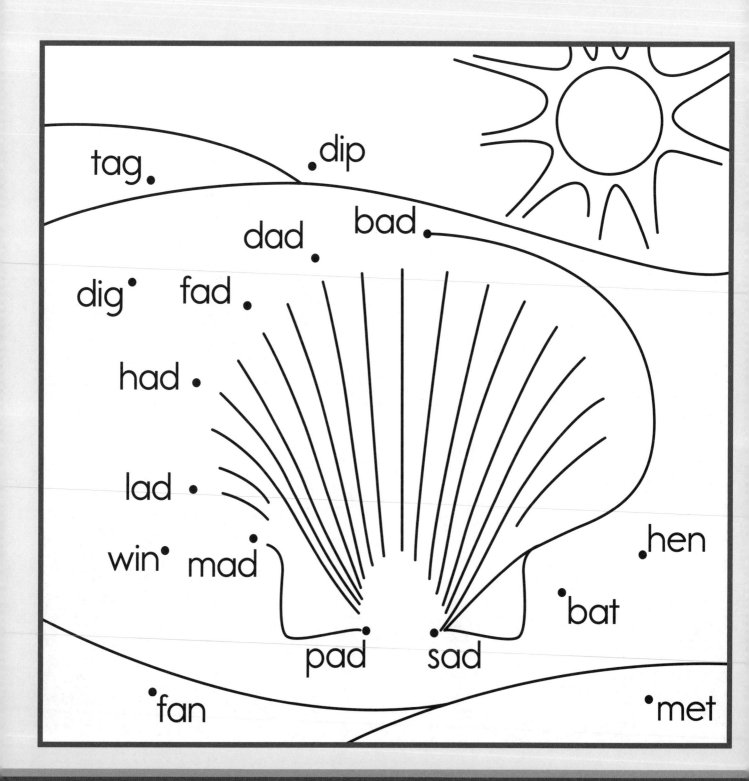

Mystery Picture

FIND the spaces with the words that sound like **ham**. COLOR those spaces blue to see the mystery picture.

HINT: You can see me in the sky at night. I am a dot of twinkling light.

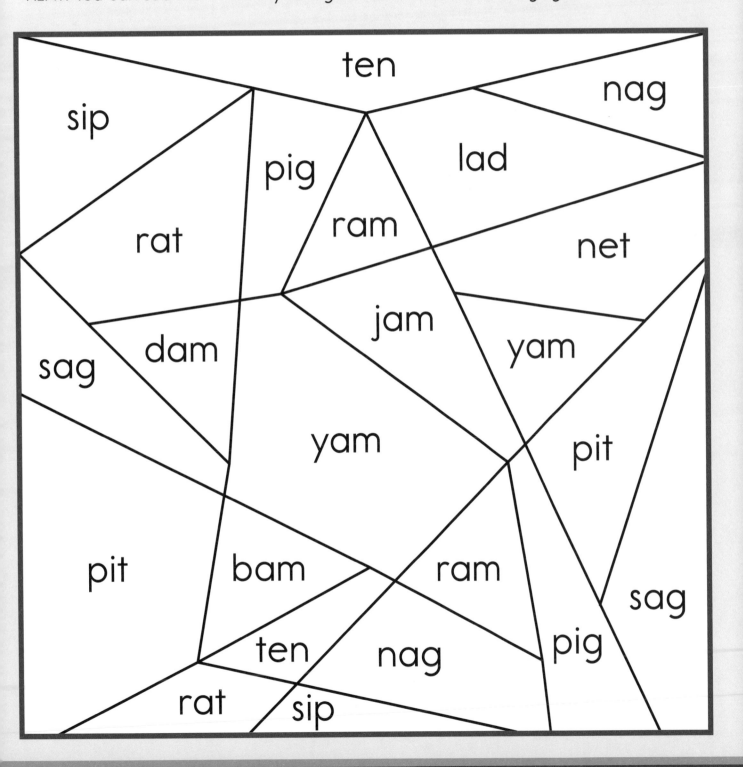

Connect the Dots

DRAW a line to connect the words that sound like **bag**. Connect them in ABC order.

HINT: Give me to a dog to chew. He will wag his tail to say, "Thank you."

Unscramble the Rhymes

UNSCRAMBLE the letters to write a rhyme for each picture.

amr   bma

_____   _____

- - - - - - - - - - - - -   - - - - - - - - - - - - -

_____   _____

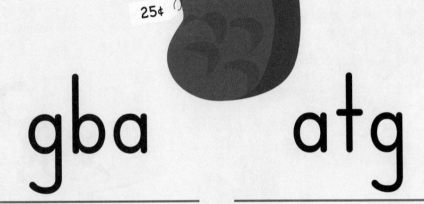

25¢

gba   atg

_____   _____

- - - - - - - - - - - - -   - - - - - - - - - - - - -

_____   _____

Hide and Seek

CIRCLE the shapes hiding in the picture.

triangle   circle   diamond   square   oval   rectangle

Make a Match

CUT OUT the words and pictures. READ the rules. PLAY the game!

Rules: 2 players
1. PLACE the cards face-down on a table.
2. TAKE TURNS turning over two cards at a time.
3. KEEP the cards when you match a picture and a word.

How many matches can you collect?

square		rectangle	
oval		circle	
triangle		diamond	

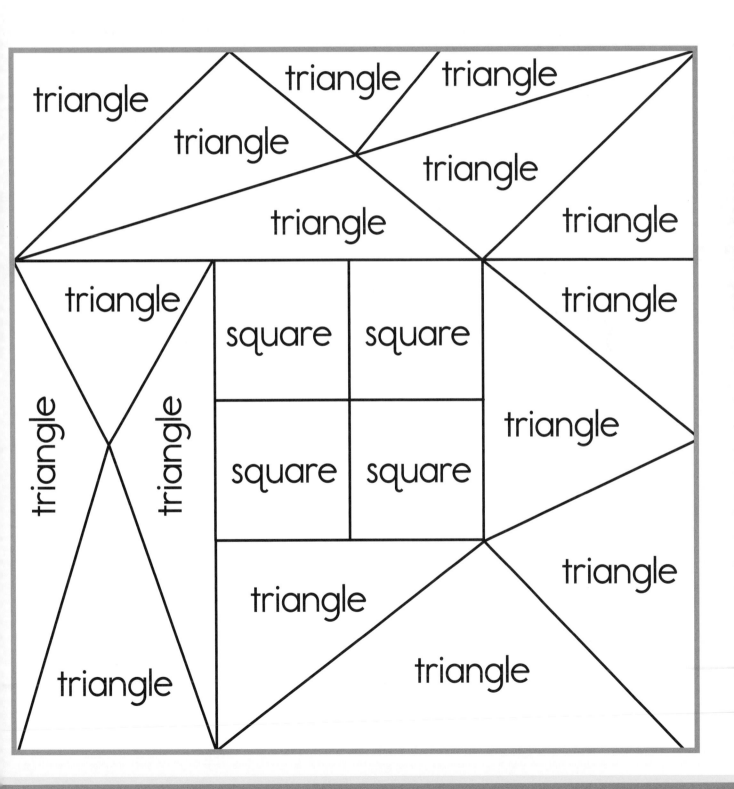

Mystery Picture

FIND the spaces with the word **square**. COLOR those spaces green to see the mystery picture.

triangle triangle triangle

triangle

triangle

triangle triangle

triangle

triangle triangle

triangle

triangle triangle

square square

square square

triangle

triangle

triangle triangle

Criss Cross

LOOK at each picture. FILL IN the missing letters to complete each shape word.

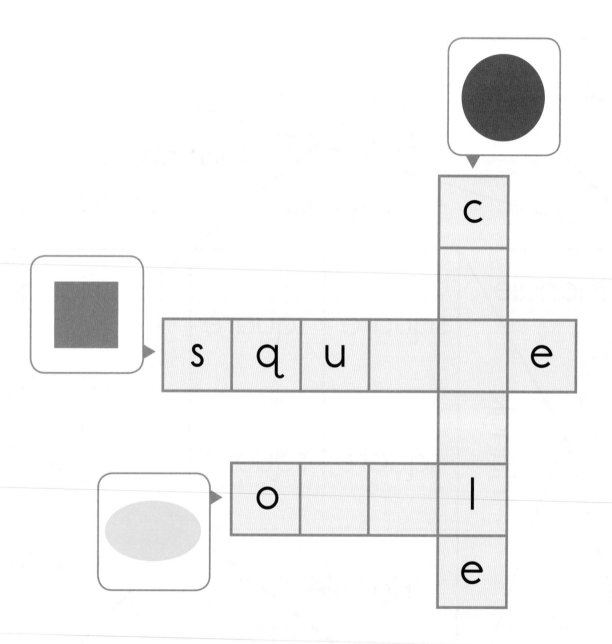

Mystery Picture

FIND the spaces with the word **diamond**. COLOR those spaces purple to see the mystery picture.

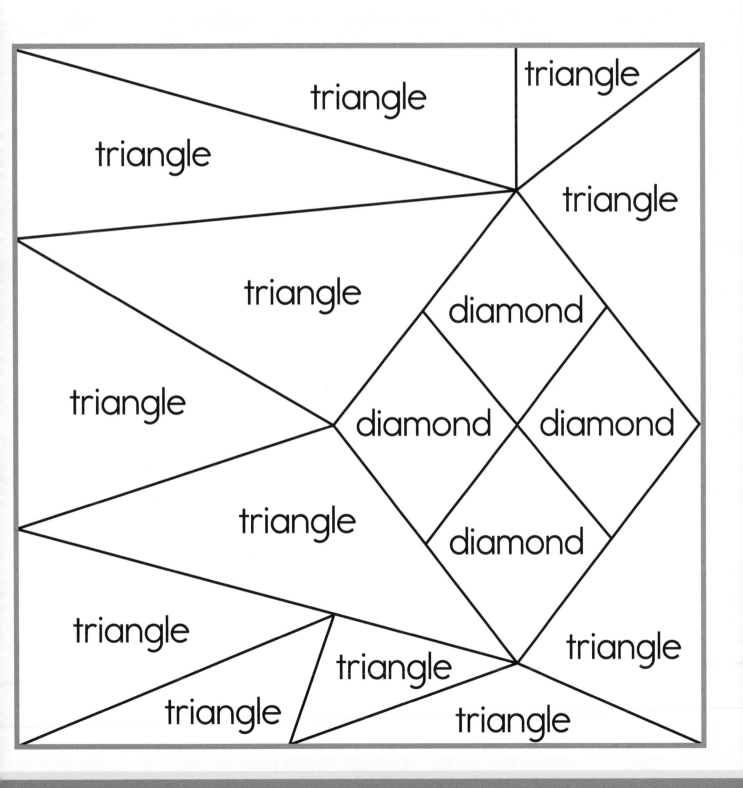

Word Hunt

CIRCLE the words in the grid that end in **-an**.
Words go across and down.

| pan | can | fan | man | ran |

b	e	z	m	p	r	i
k	d	g	w	t	a	o
p	a	n	c	s	n	h
u	q	f	c	j	l	n
m	v	x	a	e	b	y
a	u	g	n	k	r	l
n	p	d	o	m	i	c
f	w	q	b	f	a	n

Find the Path

DRAW a line through the words that end in **-an** to help the van get to the farm.

Word Hunt

CIRCLE the words in the grid that end in **-at**.
Words go across and down.

cat	rat	fat	hat	mat	sat

i	r	a	t	z	d	q
c	p	f	w	s	u	b
e	l	r	v	a	h	m
c	a	t	y	t	o	g
s	x	e	t	n	b	z
o	f	k	d	m	a	t
r	a	i	l	f	q	j
z	t	o	h	a	t	n

Find the Path

DRAW a line through the words that end in **-at** to help the bat get to the cave.

End

cat

ham   yam   lad

fat   ram   jam

                    dam   mad
        sad

rat

                    sat

        mat   Start

had

        dad

Word Hunt

CIRCLE the words in the grid that end in **-en**.
Words go across and down.

-en

| den | ten | pen | men | hen |

a	r	t	p	e	n	u
h	e	n	v	s	c	m
p	l	h	i	b	o	y
n	k	j	w	d	e	n
u	m	f	q	v	z	d
r	e	q	b	k	h	t
o	n	p	g	r	l	e
k	u	y	x	s	c	n

Find the Path

DRAW a line through the words that end in **-en** to help the hen go home.

pat

rat

sat

End

men

bat

pan

den

hat

ten

ran

hen

man

fan

can

pen **Start**

Connect the Dots

DRAW a line to connect the words that sound like **pan**. Connect them in ABC order.

HINT: Drawing pictures is what I do. I am many colors like red and blue.

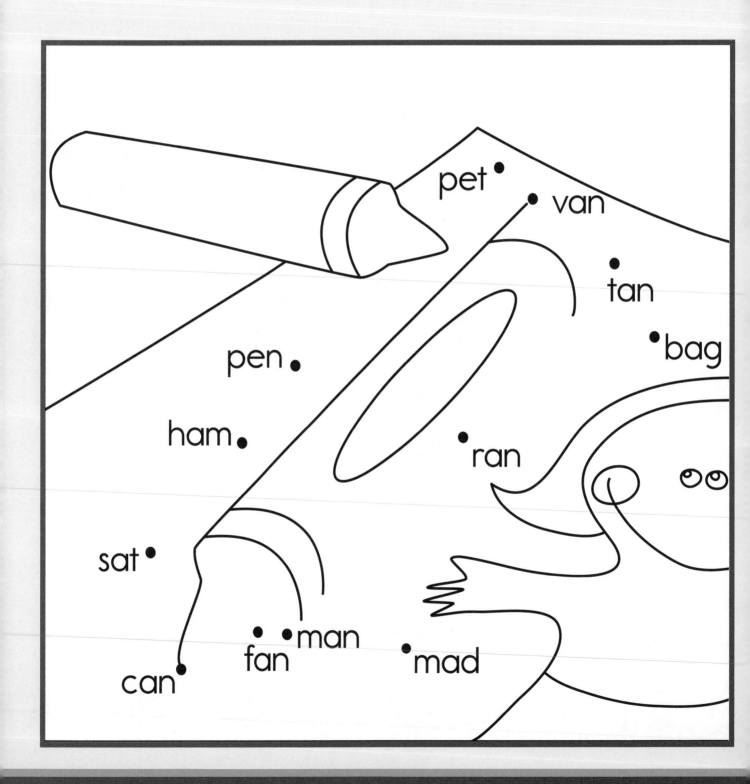

Mystery Picture

FIND the spaces with words that rhyme with **Ken**. COLOR those spaces red to see the mystery picture.

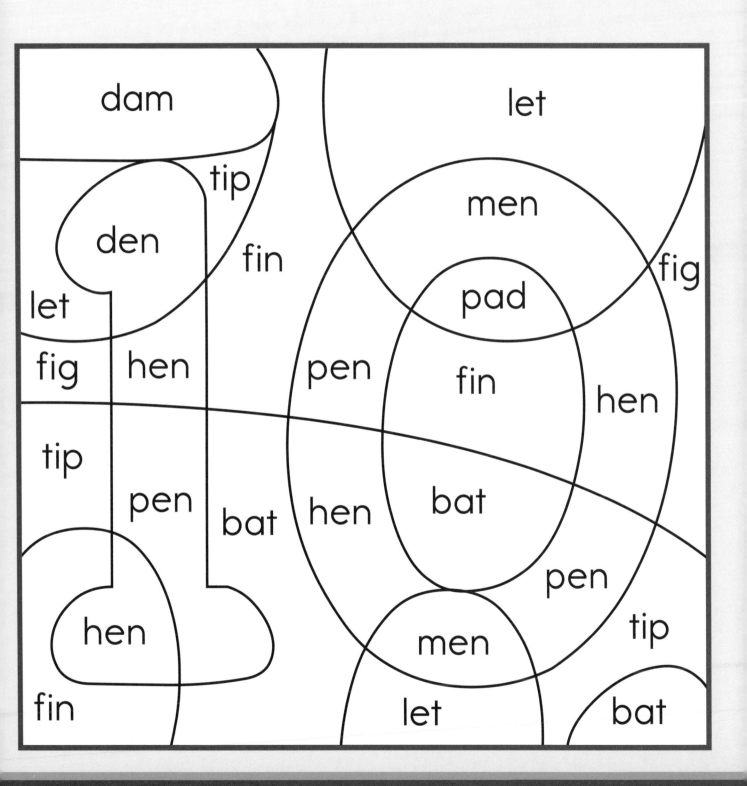

Connect the Dots

DRAW a line to connect the words that sound like **bat**. Connect them in ABC order.

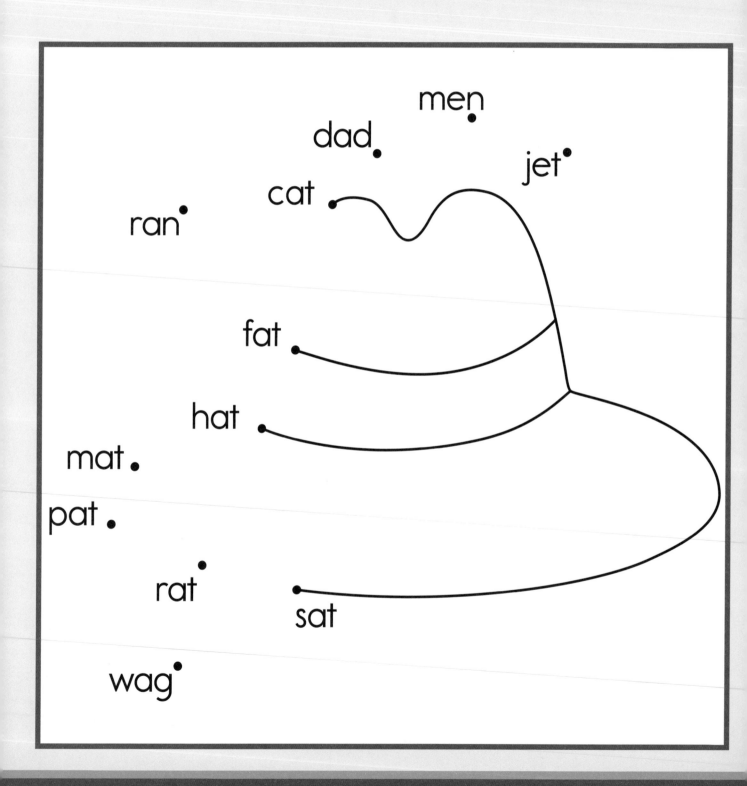

men

dad

jet

cat

ran

fat

hat

mat

pat

rat

sat

wag

Unscramble the Rhymes

UNSCRAMBLE the letters to write a rhyme for each picture.

neh   npe

atb   hta

Unscramble It

UNSCRAMBLE the letters to write the word for each animal picture.

tca cat

odg ___ ___ ___

gpi ___ ___ ___

tar ___ ___ ___

fxo ___ ___ ___

Who Am I?

MATCH each animal word to its picture.

horse

cow

bird

mouse

goat

Animals

Hide and Seek

CIRCLE the animals in the picture.

cow   horse   goat   mouse   dog   bird

Who Am I?

MATCH each animal word to its picture.

zebra

tiger

elephant

lion

monkey

Hide and Seek

CIRCLE the animals in the picture.

monkey	elephant	tiger	lion	zebra	bat

Criss Cross

LOOK at each picture. FILL IN the missing letters to complete each animal word.

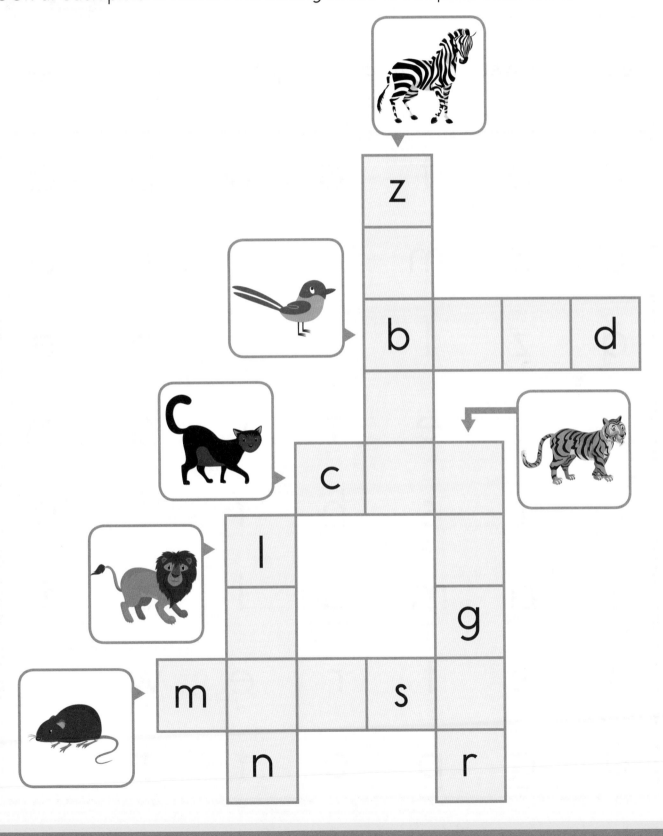

Word Endings

Word Hunt

CIRCLE the words in the grid that end in **-et**.
Words go across and down.

| pet | wet | met | jet | let | set |

p	e	t	a	w	b	d
c	k	m	i	e	r	p
q	z	l	o	t	n	e
u	j	e	t	v	a	m
r	t	s	h	f	i	e
j	q	m	u	l	s	t
s	e	t	r	e	w	z
a	g	p	o	t	t	e

Find the Path

DRAW a line through the words that end in **-et** to help the fish swim to her friends.

men

big

Start

ten

get

fig

set

dig

wig

let

jet

hen

pig

den

pen

wet

End

Word Hunt

-ig

CIRCLE the words in the grid that end in **-ig**.
Words go across and down.

| wig | pig | fig | big | dig | jig |

p	d	f	j	i	g	r
i	q	e	m	n	s	a
g	p	h	r	b	i	u
v	x	w	a	i	o	w
f	i	g	e	g	t	i
s	r	n	c	p	e	g
u	b	d	i	g	k	x
y	f	e	n	f	q	r

Find the Path

DRAW a line through the words that end in **-ig** to help the pig into the pen.

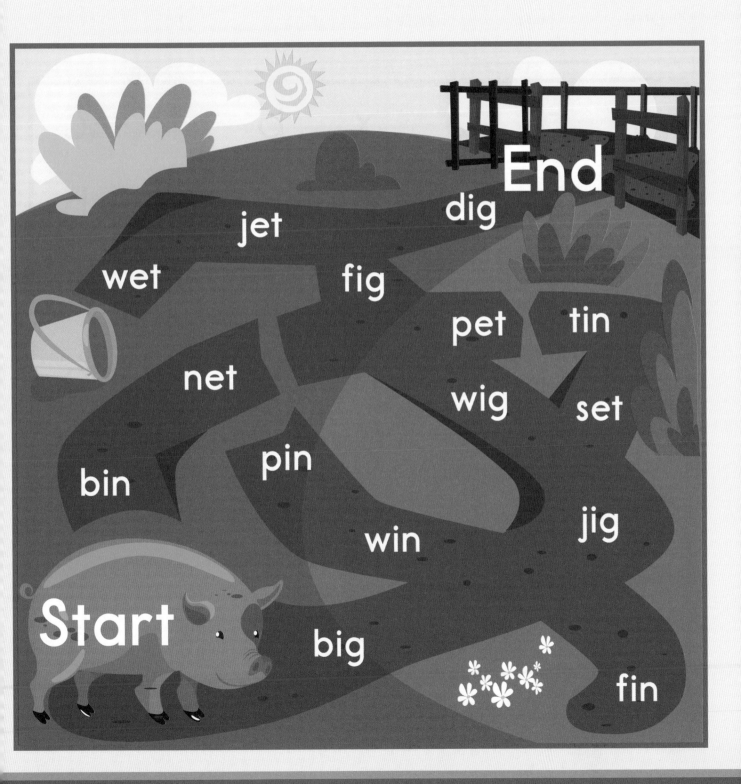

Word Hunt

CIRCLE the words in the grid that end in **-in**.
Words go across and down.

| pin | fin | win | kin | tin | bin |

a	d	z	x	b	f	c
t	y	u	p	e	i	h
i	f	v	i	t	n	s
n	g	j	n	k	r	p
q	l	m	o	e	t	w
w	i	n	y	k	f	h
a	r	v	u	i	b	k
b	i	n	s	n	q	d

Find the Path

DRAW a line through the words that end in **-in** to help the tiger through the grass.

Start

rip

fig

hip

tin

bin

fin

wig

sip

win

dig

tip

kin

pig

End

lip

Connect the Dots

DRAW a line to connect the words that sound like **pin**. Connect them in ABC order.

HINT: I am round and lots of fun. Sometimes, I make you run.

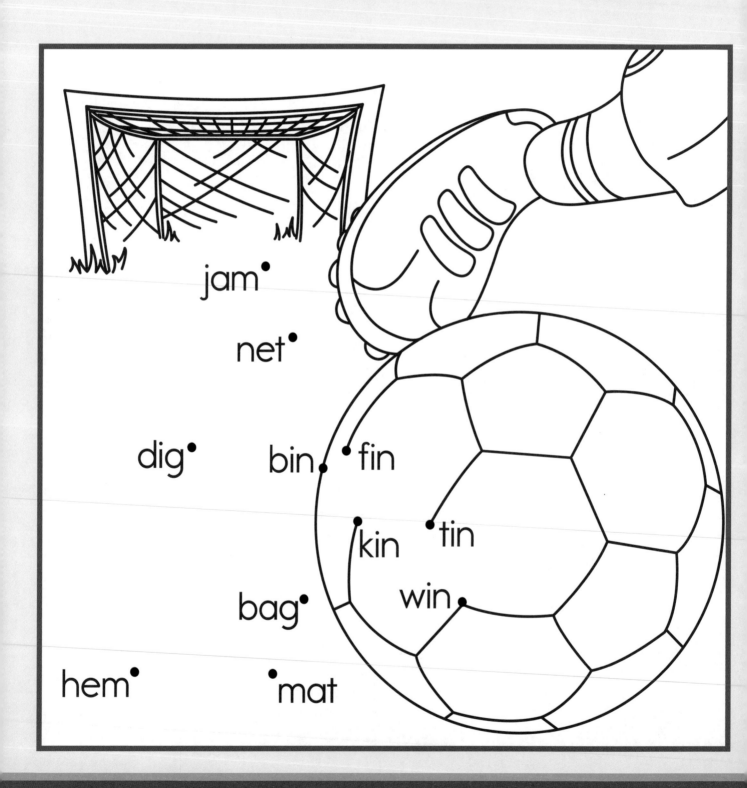

jam

net

dig   bin   fin

kin   tin

bag   win

hem   mat

Mystery Picture

FIND the spaces with words that sound like **pet**. COLOR those spaces red to see the mystery picture.

HINT: I am a fruit from a tree. I crunch when you bite into me.

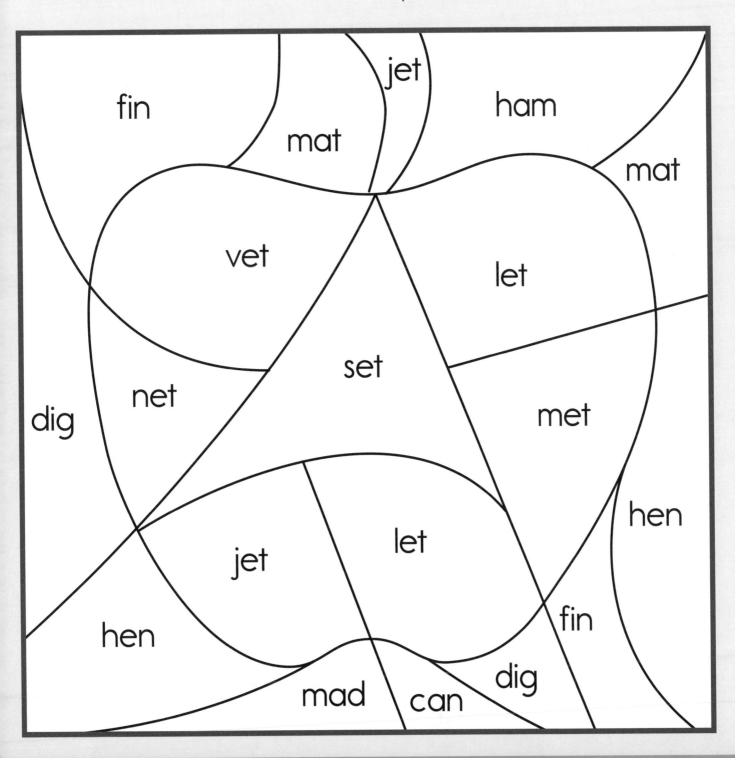

Rhyming Fun

Connect the Dots

DRAW a line to connect the words that sound like **pig**. Connect them in ABC order.

HINT: I am a shape that says, "I love you." Red is my favorite color too.

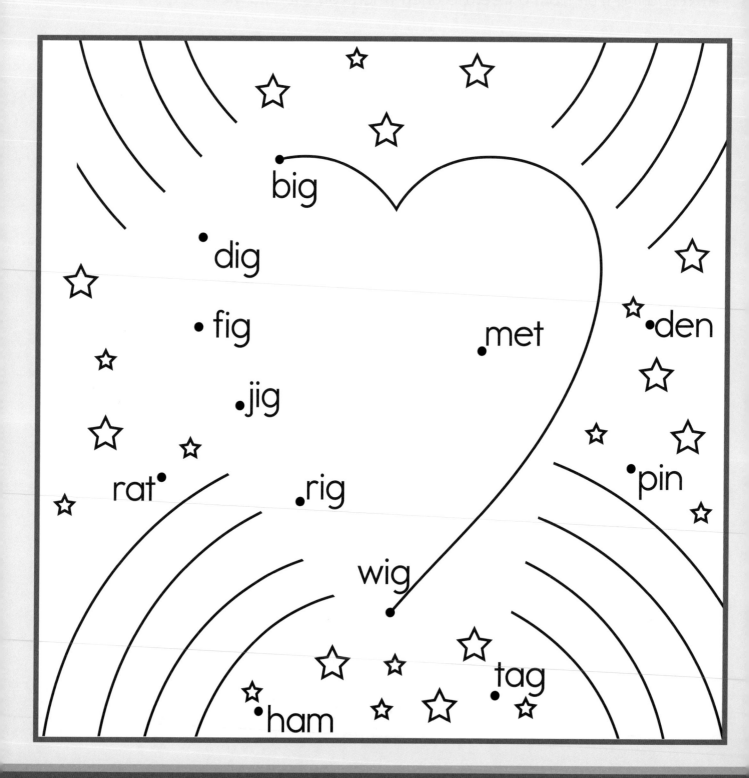

Unscramble the Rhymes

UNSCRAMBLE the letters to write a rhyme for each picture.

twe   ept

_____   _____

- - - - - -   - - - - - -

_____   _____

igb   giw

_____   _____

- - - - - -   - - - - - -

_____   _____

What to Wear?

Label the Clothing

DRAW a line from each word to an item of clothing on the boy.

mitten

pants

hat

boot

sweater

Label the Clothing

DRAW a line from each word to an item of clothing on the girl.

skirt

shirt

socks

shoes

belt

What to Wear?

Unscramble It

UNSCRAMBLE the letters to write the word for each clothing picture.

ittmen

_____
1

aht

_____
2

tspan

_____
3

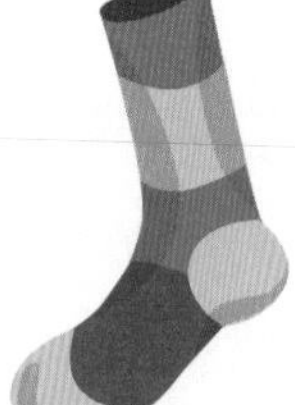

ckso

_____
4

ssdre

_____
5

Hide and Seek

FIND and CIRCLE each item of clothing in the picture.

| shoes | shirt | belt | sock | pants | hat |

What to Wear?

Word Hunt

CIRCLE each clothing word in the grid. Words go across and down.

hat   dress   mitten   boot   shirt   sweater

p	b	o	o	t	e	s
h	a	t	q	b	c	w
d	r	i	d	k	n	e
s	j	g	r	w	f	a
h	l	a	e	h	o	t
i	u	x	s	y	d	e
r	z	r	s	c	m	r
t	m	i	t	t	e	n

Criss Cross

LOOK at each picture. FILL IN the missing letters to complete the clothing words.

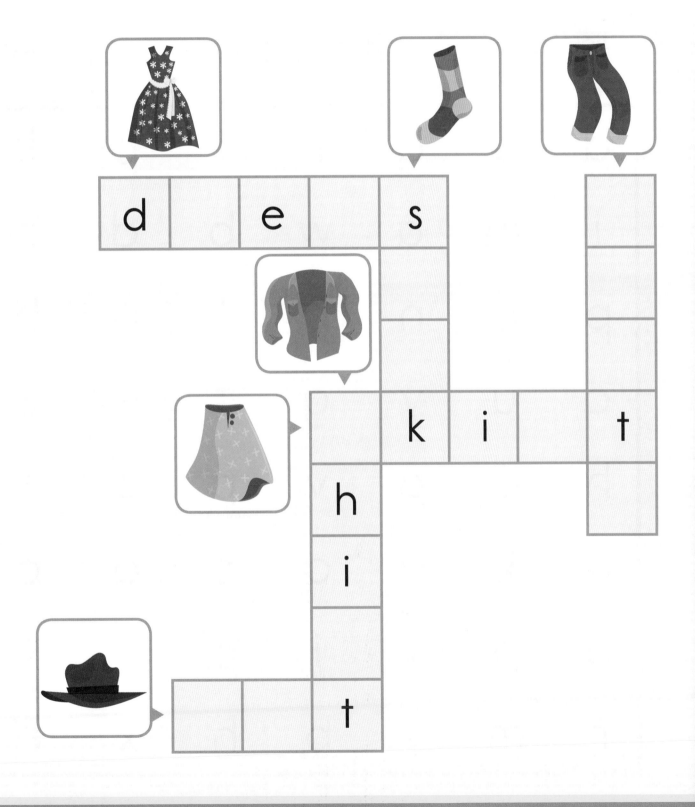

Word Hunt

-ip

CIRCLE the words in the grid that end in **-ip**.
Words go across and down.

| dip | hip | lip | rip | tip | zip |

d	o	q	r	i	p	k
i	m	a	w	b	d	r
p	o	n	p	l	u	h
c	u	y	g	i	e	z
h	i	p	v	p	s	i
w	k	u	q	c	g	p
a	p	t	i	p	j	t
r	m	y	b	h	x	e

Find the Path

FOLLOW the path marked with words ending in **-ip** to help the goat cross the bridge.

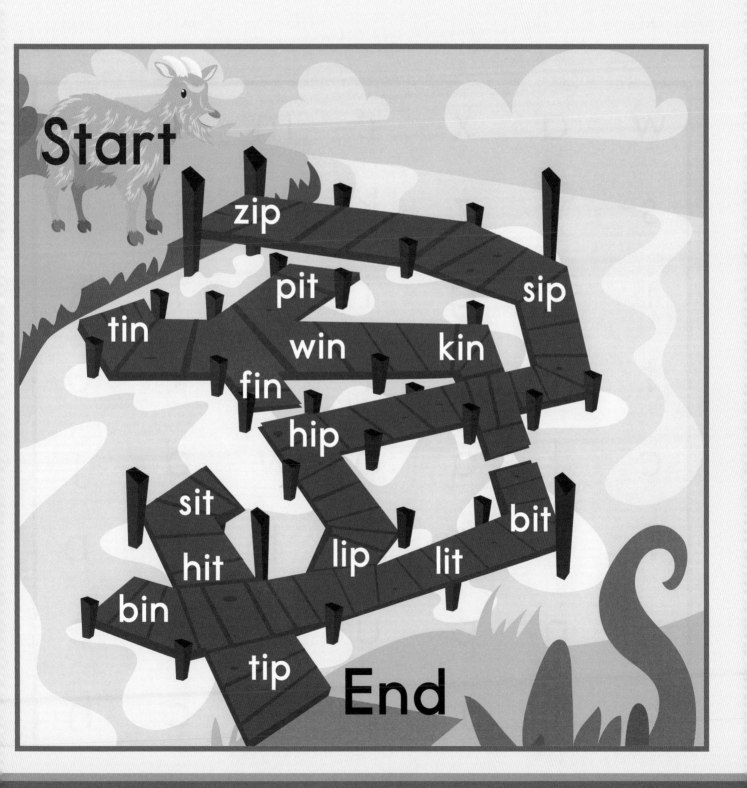

Start

zip

pit

sip

tin

win

kin

fin

hip

sit

bit

hit

lip

lit

bin

tip

End

Word Hunt

CIRCLE the words in the grid that end in **-it**.
Words go across and down.

| bit | kit | sit | fit | lit | hit |

w	a	x	r	m	b	e
s	v	z	k	h	i	n
i	y	g	i	e	t	s
t	t	f	t	b	k	u
c	l	q	o	w	d	j
f	i	t	m	l	f	r
v	n	p	u	i	b	e
h	i	t	a	t	c	h

Find the Path

FOLLOW the path marked with words ending in **-it** to help the mouse get the cheese.

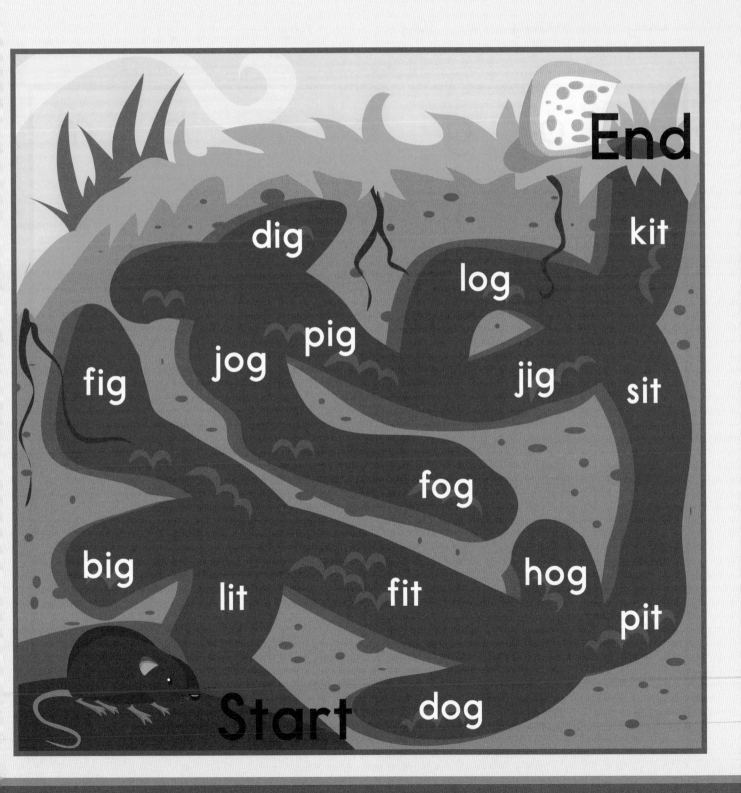

Word Hunt

-og

CIRCLE the words in the grid that end in **-og**.
Words go across and down.

| bog | dog | fog | hog | jog | log |

l	o	g	e	h	b	m
x	f	l	y	o	a	c
d	n	k	z	g	r	v
t	b	o	g	s	i	d
q	p	a	j	w	u	o
b	l	v	r	f	t	g
j	o	g	s	o	c	h
e	d	p	y	g	x	i

Find the Path

FOLLOW the path marked with words ending in **-og** to help the dog to the log.

Connect the Dots

DRAW a line to connect the words that sound like **pit**. Connect them in ABC order.

HINT: I am seen in the sky at night. I change size and my color is white.

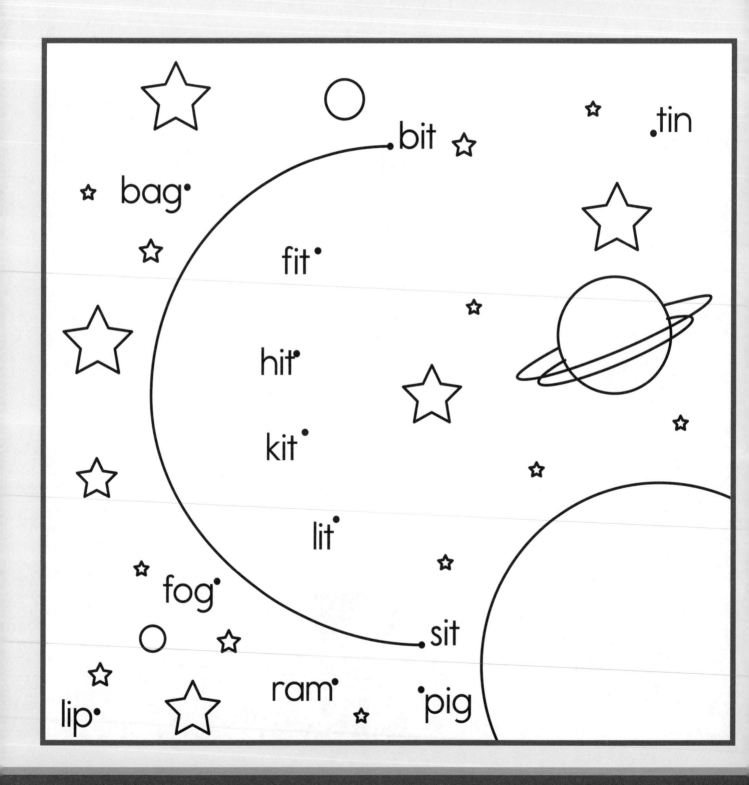

bit

.tin

bag

fit

hit

kit

lit

fog

sit

lip

ram

pig

Mystery Picture

FIND the spaces with words that sound like **dip**. COLOR those spaces yellow to see the mystery picture.

HINT: I give the day its light. I am hot and very bright.

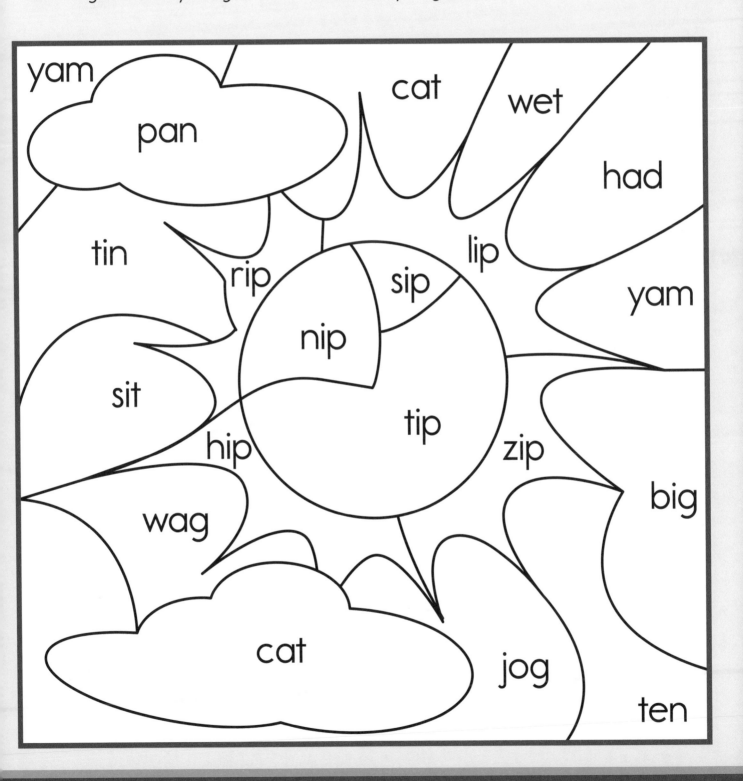

Rhyming Fun

Connect the Dots

DRAW a line to connect the words that sound like **fog**. Connect them in ABC order.

HINT: I used to be part of a tree. There's a hole inside of me.

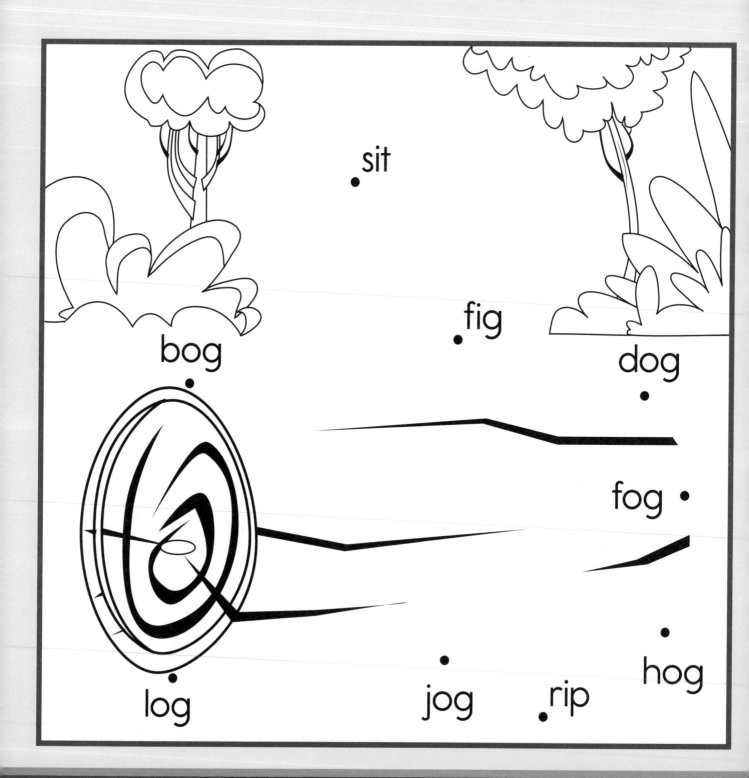

Unscramble the Rhymes

UNSCRAMBLE the letters to write a rhyme for each picture.

odg   goj

_____   _____

- - - - - - -   - - - - - - -

_____   _____

gip   jjg

_____   _____

- - - - - - -   - - - - - - -

_____   _____

The Body

Label the Parts

MATCH the words to the picture. DRAW a line from each word to the right part of the girl's face.

nose

eye

mouth

hair

ear

Label the Parts

MATCH the words to the picture. DRAW a line from each word to the right part of the boy's body.

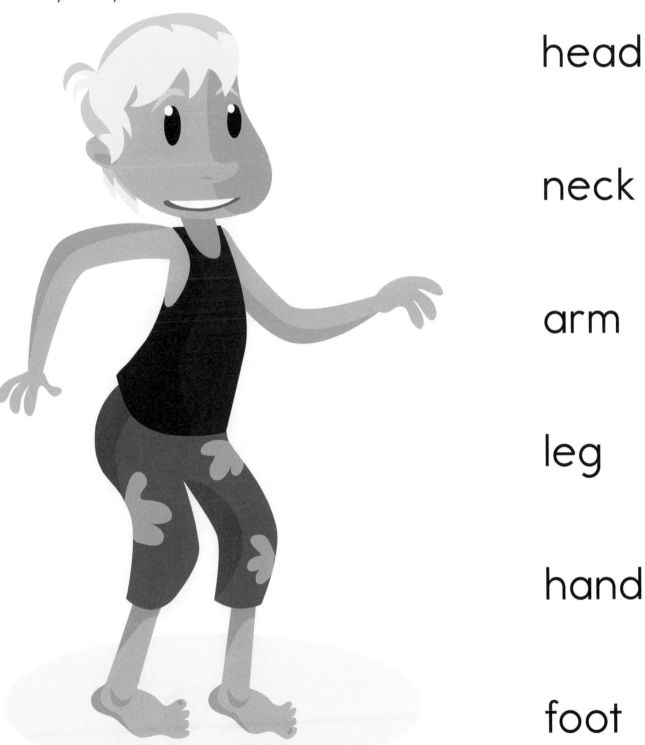

head

neck

arm

leg

hand

foot

The Body

Match Up

MATCH each word to the right picture.

hand

eye

nose

foot

ear

Make a Match

CUT OUT the words and pictures. READ the rules. PLAY the game!

Rules: 2 players
1. PLACE the cards face-down on a table.
2. TAKE TURNS turning over two cards at a time.
3. KEEP the cards when you match a picture and a word.

How many matches can you collect?

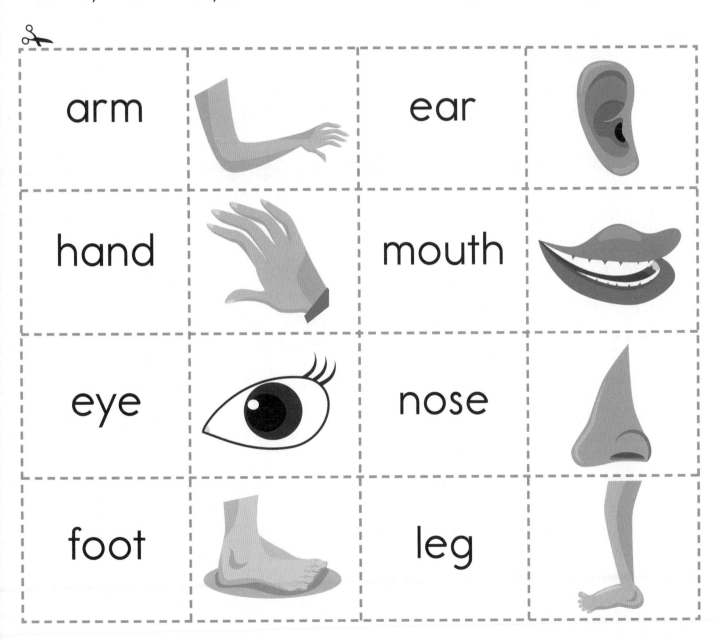

Criss Cross

LOOK at each picture. FILL IN the missing letters to complete each word.

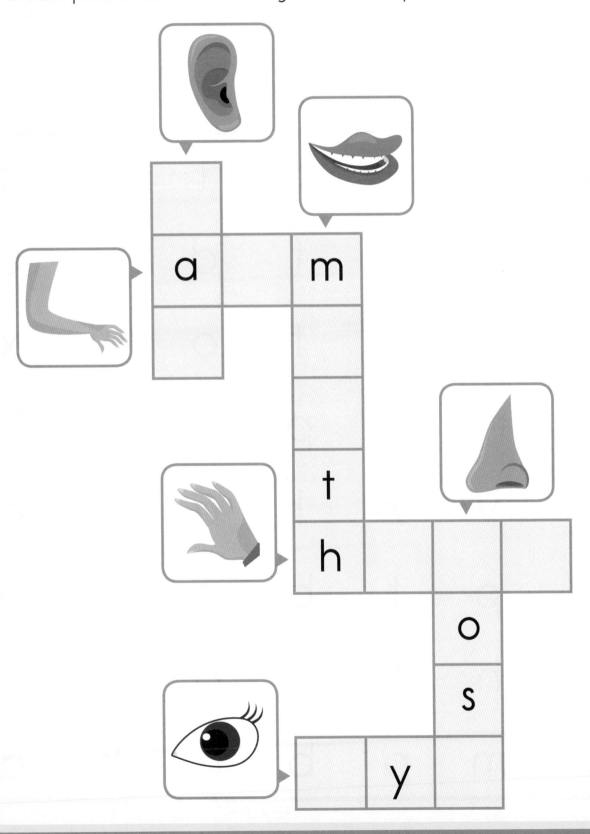

Word Hunt

CIRCLE the words in the grid that end in **-op**.
Words go across and down.

-op

| bop | hop | top | mop | pop |

e	q	r	b	l	a	s
b	o	p	f	d	m	u
c	j	n	t	o	w	x
y	m	o	p	i	g	h
k	v	z	l	a	y	o
i	p	t	b	p	e	p
f	h	o	u	o	z	s
r	m	p	b	p	k	d

Find the Path

DRAW a line through the words that end in **-op** to help the kangaroo hop to the top of the hill.

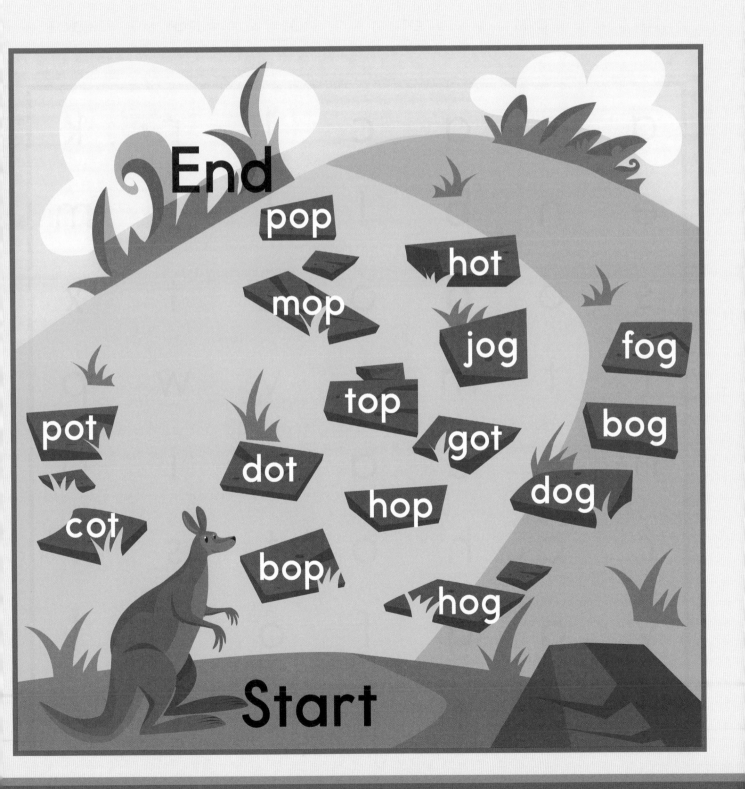

End

pop

hot

mop

jog

fog

top

bog

pot

got

dot

dog

hop

cot

bop

hog

Start

Word Hunt

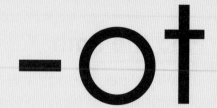

CIRCLE the words in the grid that end in **-ot**.
Words go across and down.

lot	pot	rot	hot	not	dot

a	z	q	c	l	r	k
e	n	b	l	f	o	m
s	o	d	o	u	t	x
f	t	m	t	v	w	p
h	j	u	a	p	i	o
r	c	h	o	t	s	t
y	q	g	f	o	h	l
d	o	t	t	v	f	a

Find the Path

DRAW a line through the words that end in **-ot** to help the butterfly get to the flowers.

Start

cot

dot

low

mow

mop

bow

pop

got

top

hot

bop

not

hop

row

tow

End

Word Hunt

CIRCLE the words in the grid that end in **-ow**.
Words go across and down.

bow	low	mow	row	tow

a	e	z	x	d	b	h
r	y	u	t	e	o	c
o	f	r	o	n	w	p
w	g	v	w	j	k	w
i	l	m	h	e	t	s
m	o	w	y	l	f	h
a	r	v	u	o	b	k
t	n	i	s	w	q	d

Find the Path

DRAW a line through the words that end in **-ow** to help the girl row the boat to shore.

Start

rot

bow

pot

tow   cub

low

hot

row

hub

sub

got

tub

rub   mow

not

End

Connect the Dots

DRAW a line to connect the words that sound like **pop**. Connect them in ABC order.

HINT: I like to climb to the **top** of these.

Mystery Picture

FIND the spaces with words that sound like **hot**. COLOR those spaces orange to see the mystery picture.

HINT: I am orange and fun to munch. I am a good part of lunch.

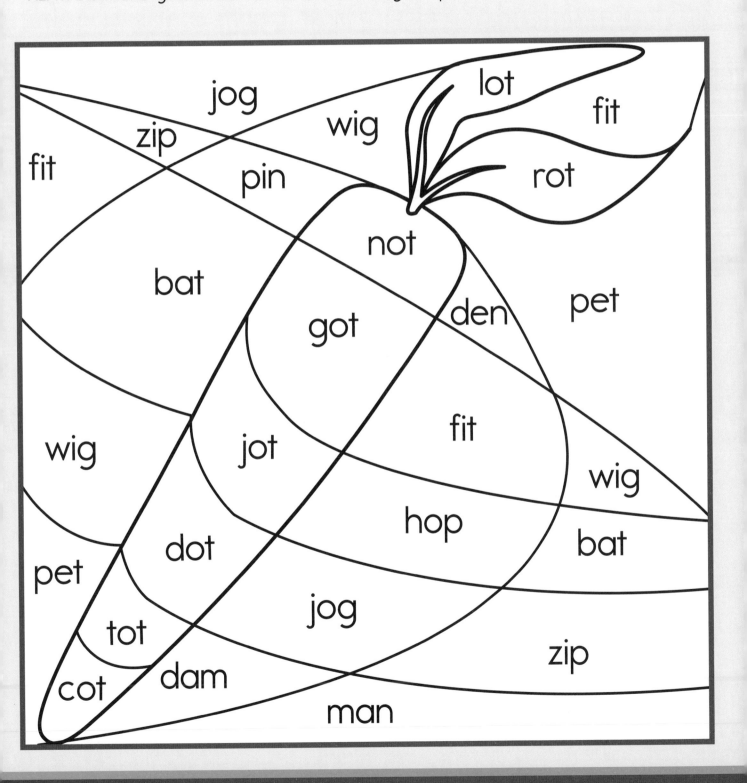

Rhyming Fun

Connect the Dots

DRAW a line to connect the words that sound like **row**. Connect them in ABC order.

HINT: The wind will help you go, so you don't have to **row**.

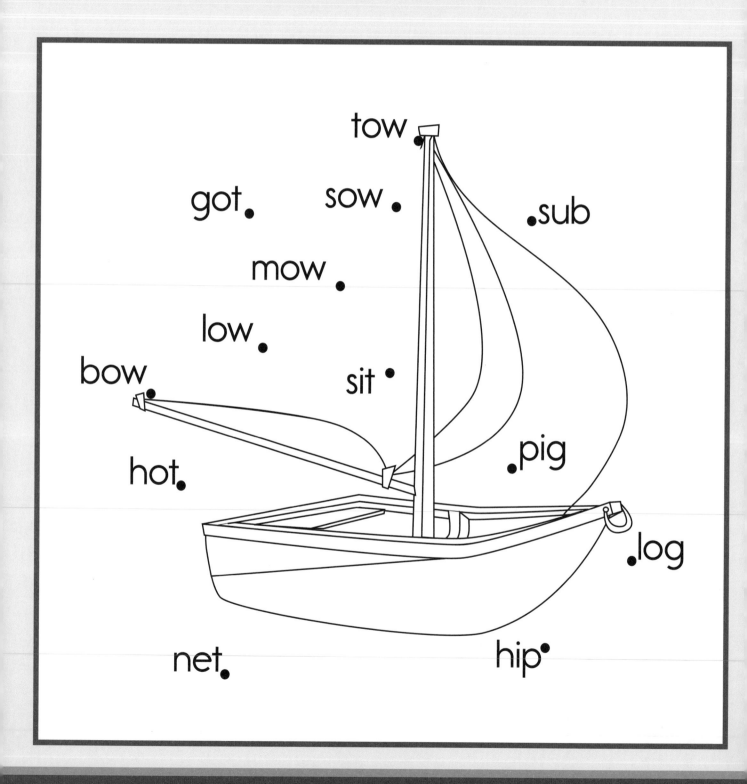

tow

got

sow

.sub

mow

low

bow

sit

.pig

hot

.log

net

hip

Unscramble the Rhymes

UNSCRAMBLE the letters to write a rhyme for each picture.

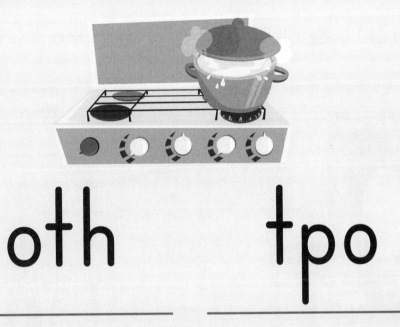

oth

tpo

wbo

wor

Food

Hide and Seek

LOOK at the words. FIND and CIRCLE each one in the picture.

egg   carrot   apple   pizza   banana   bread   cake

Unscramble It

UNSCRAMBLE the letters to write the word for each picture.

gge

_____
1

pplea

_____
2

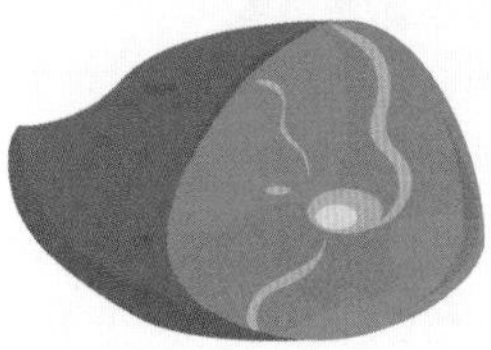

ahm

_____
3

anaban

_____
4

keca

_____
5

What Am I?

MATCH each word to its picture.

bread

lemon

tomato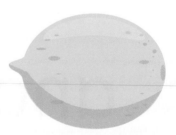

carrot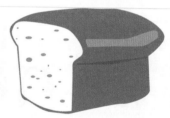

pizza

Make a Match

CUT OUT the words and pictures. READ the rules. PLAY the game!

Rules: 2 players
1. PLACE the cards face-down on a table.
2. TAKE TURNS turning over two cards at a time.
3. KEEP the cards when you match a picture and a word.

How many matches can you collect?

Criss Cross

LOOK at each picture. FILL IN the missing letters to complete each food word.

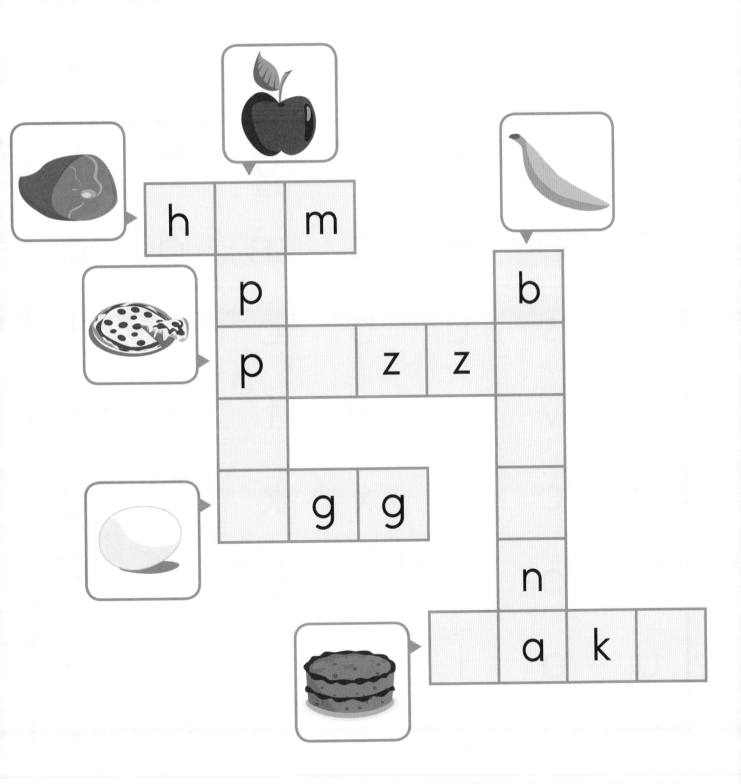

Word Hunt

CIRCLE the words in the grid that end in **-ub**.
Words go across and down.

cub	hub	rub	sub	tub

a	l	t	t	u	b	k
s	p	e	b	m	o	q
j	s	u	b	c	h	i
g	v	d	w	f	z	r
u	c	r	x	k	i	u
c	o	h	u	b	y	b
u	a	l	v	d	x	e
b	d	n	r	z	u	f

Find the Path

DRAW a line through the words that end in **-ub** to help the cub find his mom.

Word Endings

Word Hunt

CIRCLE the words in the grid that end in **-ug**.
Words go across and down.

-ug

bug	dug	hug	mug	rug	tug

c	f	m	o	x	d	p
b	e	n	h	i	u	w
u	h	i	u	t	g	q
g	a	l	g	d	w	b
k	n	v	i	r	u	z
r	u	g	a	m	f	l
e	d	s	x	u	q	g
t	u	g	z	g	e	h

Find the Path

DRAW a line through the words that end in **-ug** to help the bug cross the rug.

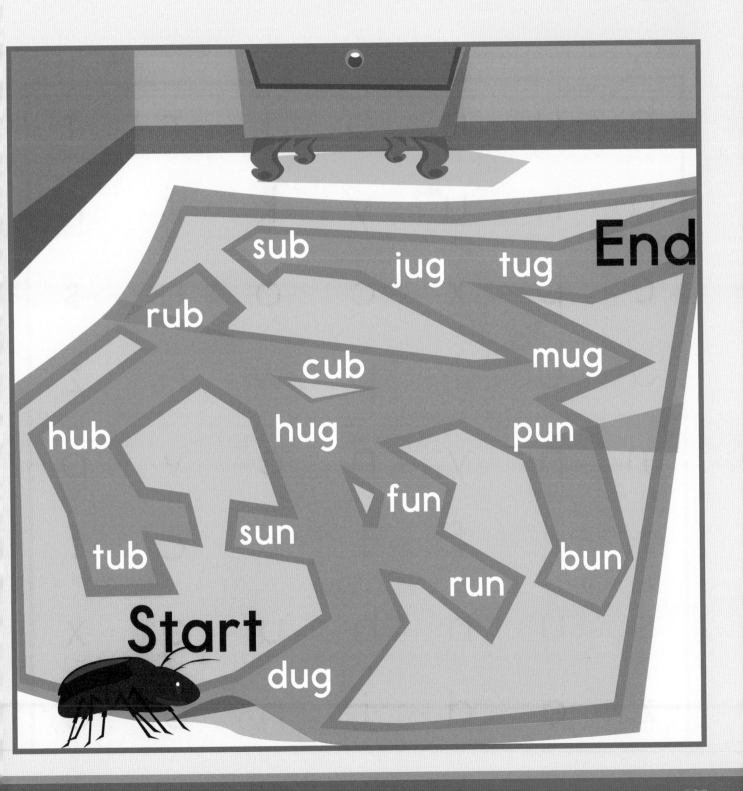

End

sub

jug   tug

rub

mug

cub

hub   hug   pun

fun

sun

tub   bun

run

Start

dug

Word Endings

Word Hunt

CIRCLE the words in the grid that end in **-un**.
Words go across and down.

| bun | fun | run | sun | pun |

b	u	n	g	i	r	t
a	h	u	y	k	f	n
c	p	x	q	o	u	s
d	u	l	p	w	n	z
m	n	y	n	e	v	p
t	r	f	l	r	c	f
s	u	n	h	u	q	x
z	a	d	i	n	b	e

Find the Path

DRAW a line through the words that end in **-un** to help the boy run the race.

Start

bug

hug

sun

hut

tug

bun

nut

but

cut

rug

rut

fun

mug

run

pun

FINISH LINE

End

Word Hunt

CIRCLE the words in the grid that end in **-ut**.
Words go across and down.

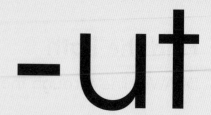

| cut | gut | hut | nut | rut |

a	z	q	y	c	i	t
s	l	p	v	u	k	w
r	u	t	o	t	r	n
b	f	m	h	e	x	g
t	g	d	k	v	i	u
o	l	n	s	h	z	t
n	u	t	q	u	e	r
y	w	a	m	t	b	u

Find the Path

DRAW a line through the words that end in **-ut** to help the squirrel get the nut.

End

rut

bun   got

dot

pun

pot   nut

but

hot

sun

run   fun

cot

hut

cut

Start

Rhyming Fun

Unscramble the Rhymes

UNSCRAMBLE the letters to write a rhyme for each picture.

buc   usb

_____   _____

- - - - - - -   - - - - - - -

_____   _____

bgu   utg

_____   _____

- - - - - - -   - - - - - - -

_____   _____

Connect the Dots

DRAW a line to connect the words that sound like **rug**. Connect them in ABC order.

fog

bag

hug

ram

dug

mug

bug

rug

tug

pig

Rhyming Fun

Color by Rhyme

COLOR each part of the picture.

 = words that sound like **tug**   = words that sound like **tub**   = words that sound like **run**   = words that sound like **hut**

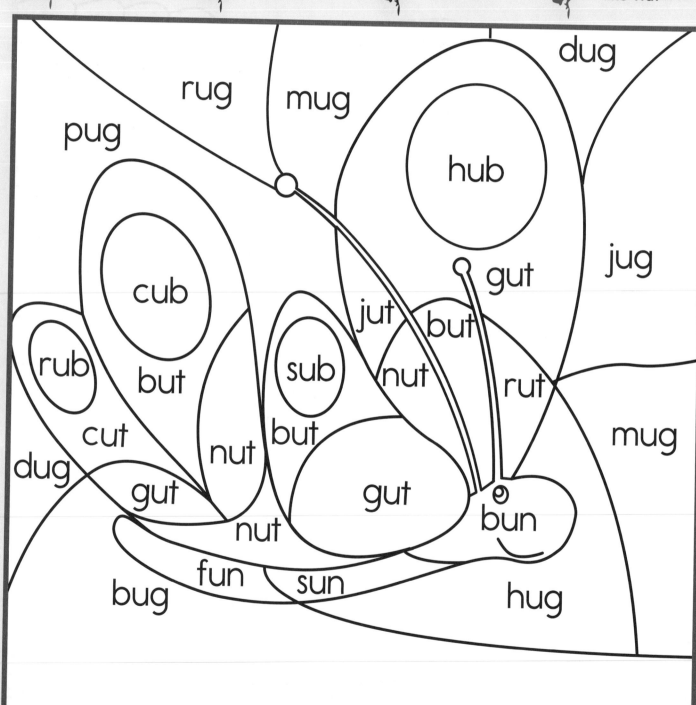

Unscramble the Rhymes

UNSCRAMBLE the letters to write a rhyme for each picture.

usn   nuf

_____   _____

- - - - - - - - - -   - - - - - - - - - -

_____   _____

ctu   ntu

_____   _____

- - - - - - - - - -   - - - - - - - - - -

_____   _____

Answers

Page 210

Page 211

Page 212

Page 213

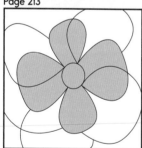

Page 214

a	z	q	c	l	h	k
e	b	n	s	a	f	m
s	a	c	a	f	u	m
f	d	m	d	v	v	d
h	j	u	o	p	i	s
r	c	m	a	d	i	d
y	q	g	f	o	e	l
p	a	d	t	v	b	a

Page 215

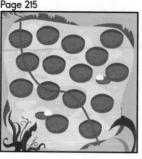

Page 216

a	e	z	x	d	s	h
w	y	u	r	a	a	c
a	c	r	a	d	g	p
g	b	v	g	j	k	w
i	l	m	h	e	t	s
b	a	g	y	t	f	h
o	r	v	u	a	b	k
t	n	i	s	g	q	d

Page 217

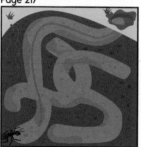

Page 218

h	a	m	e	y	b	d
c	k	m	i	a	r	p
q	z	x	o	m	n	e
u	d	a	m	n	o	j
u	r	t	s	h	f	i	a
j	q	c	u	l	s	m
r	a	m	r	e	w	z
a	g	p	o	t	t	e

Page 219

Page 220

Page 221

Page 222

Page 223
ram bam, bag tag

Page 224

Page 227

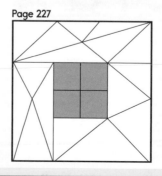

Page 228

```
            c
            i
s q u a r e c
            l
    o v a l e
            e
```

Page 229

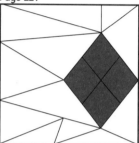

Page 230

b	e	z	m	p	r	i
k	d	g	w	t	a	o
p	a	n	c	s	n	h
u	q	f	c	j	l	n
m	v	x	a	e	b	y
a	u	g	n	k	r	l
n	p	d	o	m	i	c
f	w	q	b	f	a	n

Page 231

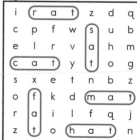

Page 232

i	r	a	t	z	d	q
c	p	f	w	s	u	b
e	l	r	v	a	h	m
c	a	t	y	t	o	g
s	x	e	t	n	b	z
o	f	k	d	m	a	t
r	a	i	l	f	q	j
z	t	o	h	a	t	n

Page 233

Page 238

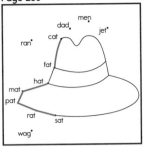

Page 244

Page 249

Page 234

Page 239

hen pen, bat hat

Page 240

cat, dog, pig, rat, fox

Page 241

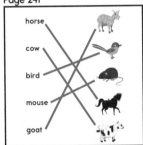

Page 245

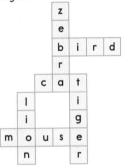

Page 250

Page 235

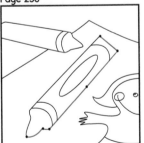

Page 236

Page 242

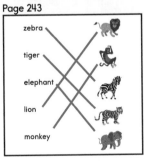

Page 243

Page 246

Page 247

Page 248

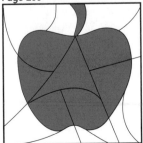

Page 237

Page 251

Page 252

Page 253

Answers

Page 254

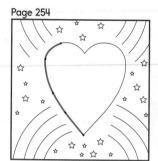

Page 255

wet pet, big wig

Page 256

mitten
pants
hat
boot
sweater

Pages 257

skirt
shirt
socks
shoes
belt

Page 258

1. mitten
2. hat
3. pants
4. sock
5. dress

Page 259

Page 260

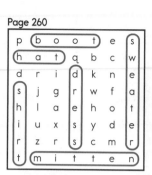

p	b	o	o	t	e	s
h	a	t	q	b	c	w
d	r	i	d	k	n	e
s	j	g	d	w	f	a
h	l	a	r	h	o	t
i	u	x	e	y	d	e
r	z	r	s	c	m	r
t	m	i	t	t	e	n

Page 261

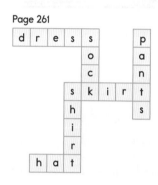

d r e s s   p
        o   a
        c   n
    s k i r t
    h   s
    i
h a t

Page 262

d	o	q	r	i	p	k
i	m	a	w	b	d	r
p	o	n	p	l	u	h
c	u	y	g	i	e	z
h	i	p	v	p	s	i
w	k	u	q	c	g	p
a	p	t	i	p	j	t
r	m	y	b	h	x	e

Page 263

Page 264

w	a	x	r	m	b	e
s	v	z	k	h	i	n
i	y	g	i	e	t	s
t	t	f	t	b	k	u
c	l	q	o	w	d	j
f	i	t	m	l	f	r
v	n	p	u	i	t	e
h	i	t	a	t	c	h

Page 265

Page 266

l	o	g	e	h	b	m
x	f	l	y	o	a	c
d	n	k	z	g	r	v
t	b	o	g	r	i	d
q	p	a	j	w	c	o
b	l	v	r	f	o	g
j	o	g	s	o	c	h
e	d	p	y	g	x	i

Page 267

Page 268

Page 269

Page 270

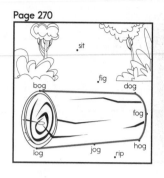

sit
fig
bog
dog
fog
log
jog
rip
hog

Page 271

dog jog, pig jig

Page 272

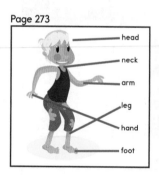

nose
eye
mouth
hair
ear

Page 273

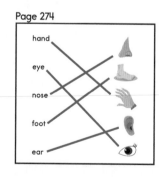

head
neck
arm
leg
hand
foot

Page 274

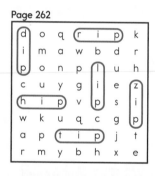

hand
eye
nose
foot
ear

308

Answers

Page 277

e					
a	r	m			
r		o			
		u			
		t			
		h	a	n	d
				o	
				s	
		e	y	e	

Page 278

e	q	r	b	l	a	s
b	**o**	**p**	f	d	m	u
c	j	n	t	o	w	x
y	**m**	**o**	**p**	i	g	**h**
k	v	z	l	a	y	**o**
i	p	**t**	b	**p**	e	**p**
f	h	**o**	u	**o**	z	s
r	m	**p**	b	**p**	k	d

Page 279

Page 280

a	z	q	c	l	**r**	k
e	**n**	b	**l**	f	**o**	m
s	**o**	d	**o**	u	**t**	x
f	**t**	m	**t**	v	w	**p**
h	j	u	a	p	i	**o**
r	c	**h**	**o**	**t**	s	**t**
y	q	g	f	o	h	l
d	**o**	**t**	t	v	f	a

Page 281

Page 282

a	e	z	x	d	**b**	h
r	y	u	**t**	e	**o**	c
o	f	r	**o**	n	**w**	p
w	g	v	**w**	j	k	w
i	l	m	h	e	t	s
m	**o**	**w**	y	**l**	f	h
a	r	v	u	**o**	b	k
t	n	i	s	**w**	q	d

Page 283

Page 284

Page 285

Page 286

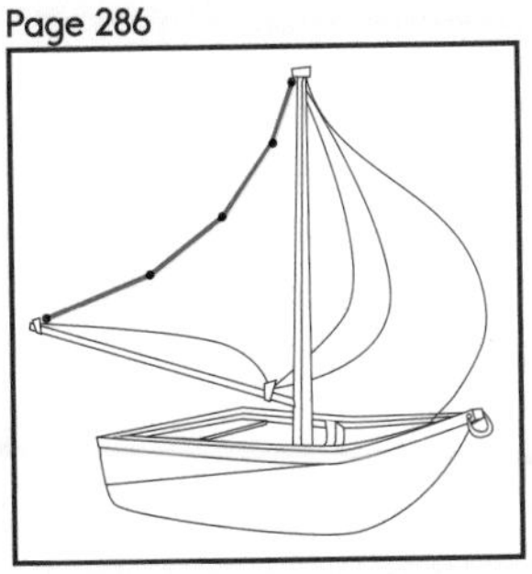

Page 287

hot pot, bow row

Page 288

Restaurant

Page 289

1. egg
2. apple
3. ham
4. banana
5. cake

Page 290

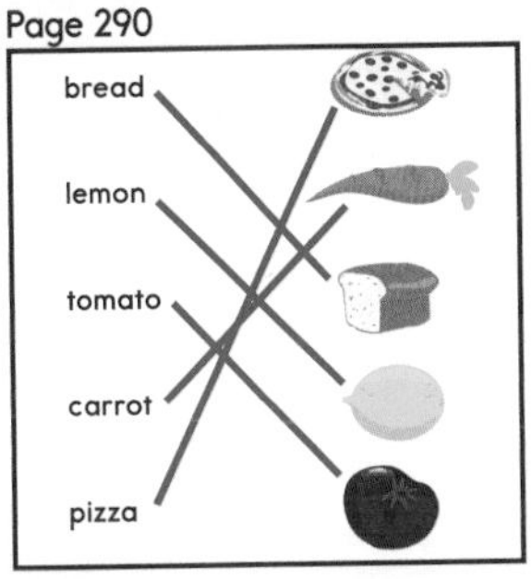
bread
lemon
tomato
carrot
pizza

Page 293

h	a	m					
	p				b		
	p	i	z	z	a		
	l				n		
	e	g	g		a		
					n		
				c	a	k	e

Page 294

a	l	t	**t**	**u**	**b**	k
s	p	e	b	m	o	q
j	**s**	**u**	**b**	c	h	i
g	v	d	w	f	z	**r**
u	c	r	x	k	i	**u**
c	o	**h**	**u**	**b**	y	**b**
u	a	l	v	d	x	e
b	d	n	r	z	u	f

Page 295

Page 296

c	f	m	o	x	**d**	p
b	e	n	**h**	i	**u**	w
u	h	i	**u**	t	**g**	q
g	a	l	**g**	d	w	b
k	n	v	i	r	u	z
r	**u**	**g**	a	**m**	f	l
e	d	s	x	**u**	q	g
t	**u**	**g**	z	**g**	e	h

Page 297

Page 298

b	**u**	**n**	g	i	r	t
a	h	u	y	k	**f**	n
c	**p**	x	q	o	**u**	s
d	**u**	l	p	w	**n**	z
m	**n**	y	n	e	v	p
t	r	f	l	**r**	c	f
s	**u**	**n**	h	**u**	q	x
z	a	d	i	**n**	b	e

Page 299

Answers

Page 300

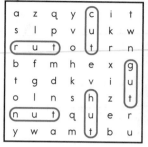

Page 301

Page 302
cub sub, bug tug

Page 303

Page 304

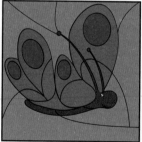

Page 305
sun fun, cut nut